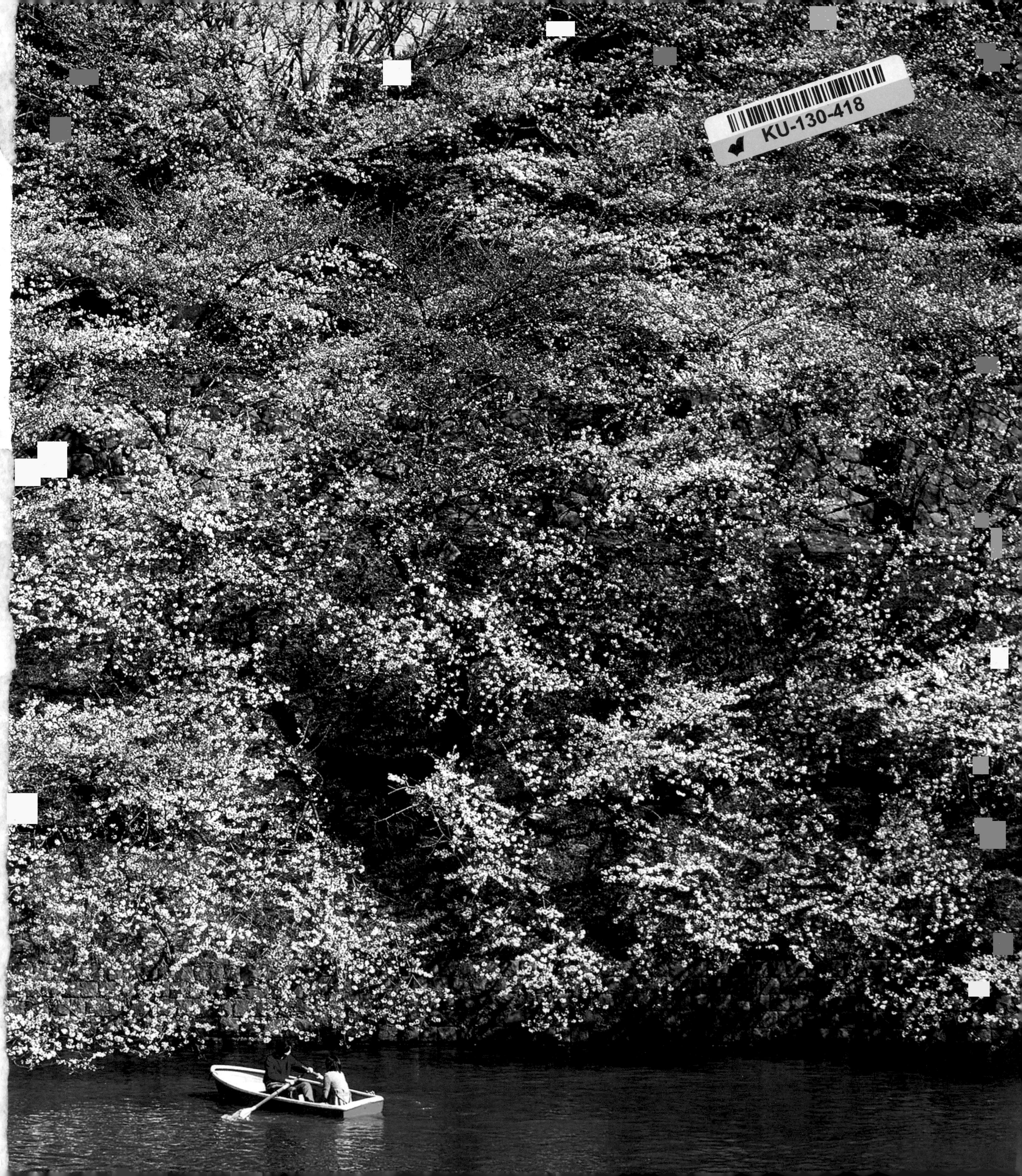

Lake Garden, Taiping, Perak

Mulu National Park, Sarawak

Taman Negara, Pahang

Fraser's Hill, Pahang

# MESSAGE FROM THE HON.
# DATO' SRI MOHD. NAJIB TUN HAJI ABDUL RAZAK

PRIME MINISTER OF MALAYSIA

A beautiful garden gives soul to a modern city, respite to those who populate such cities, and a sense of peaceful balance to the rapid development of a nation. Thus, the preservation of nature, especially in times of such great development as we are in now, is of paramount importance.

The Government of Malaysia is fully aware of the need to strike an optimal balance between development needs and the preservation of the environment. In response, we have emphasized the care and conservation of the environment in the nation's development plans and encouraged functional landscape development such as the greening of cities, development of public parks and recreational areas, and the conservation and maintenance of natural assets.

In addition, at the 2009 United Nations Climate Change Conference in Copenhagen, the Government of Malaysia set voluntary national indicators to measure our progress in climate action; one of them is that we remain committed to ensure at least 50% of our land area remain as forests as pledged in the Rio Summit.

On a personal note, I am very much heartened to know that in many parts of the world, there still exist large green lungs of flora and fauna to ensure the cycle of life continues. Whether they are gardens created by man or by nature, or perhaps both, these pockets of greenery serve as a constant reminder of what we must treasure most even as we progress into the future.

I am pleased that three of Malaysia's own garden paradise were deemed fit to be included in this beautiful publication. I believe that these gardens were selected based on the unique properties in their design, landscaping, and horticultural significance that truly reflect the identity of Malaysia.

I hope that you will enjoy looking through these pages and may the gardens evoke in you a sense of wonder and enchantment, and inspire you to preserve a harmonious balance in your own personal paradise.

# MESSAGE FROM THE HON. DATO' SRI DR. NG YEN YEN

MINISTER OF TOURISM, MALAYSIA

Malaysia is naturally blessed with 8,000 species of flowering plants, 3,000 species of trees, 1,000 species of orchids, 300 species of palms and 60 species of bamboos in our evergreen tropical landscape. It's certainly a great "palette of colours" to have in designing a unique brand of Malaysian gardens and parks.

Although there is no exact record of the history of gardens in Malaysia, its existence and beauty have been described in many classic Malay writings from the 18th and 19th centuries. In them, gardens that surrounded the Malacca palace in the 15th century were described in great detail. Among the earliest mention of gardens in Malaysia was by a Buddhist pilgrim who came across the royal garden of an old Malay kingdom in 609 A.D. However, the first public garden in the country was introduced by the British in 1890 and is known till today as the Lake Gardens. Today, various beautifully designed gardens can be found all over Malaysia.

I am a firm believer that a simple walk in a beautiful garden can help reduce stress and refresh our weary spirit. It is a perfect way to balance our hectic lifestyles, yet there is still a lack of awareness among the locals of the vast benefits that gardens can offer to our society. As I see it, the level of appreciation of natural beauty is higher among the society in developed countries.

Therefore, in an effort to generate awareness towards Malaysia's enchanting gardens and parks, the Ministry of Tourism Malaysia has created a special garden tourism package to attract gardens enthusiasts from all over the world. Among the parks and gardens that will be promoted are Lake Gardens in Kuala Lumpur; Taman Warisan Pertanian, the Botanical Garden and Wawasan Park in Putrajaya; the Bukit Cahaya Sri Alam Agricultural Park in Shah Alam; Fraser's Hill, Taiping Lake Garden in Perak; Venice of Malaysia, Melati Lake and Gua Kelam in Perlis; Penang Hill, Penang Botanical Gardens, Tropical Fruit Farm and Tropical Spice Garden in Penang.

I am grateful to the Chelsea Pensioners' Appeal for their willingness to publish a special edition of Paradise Found – Journeys Though Noble Gardens of Asia as a show of support to our garden tourism package. The fact that the original edition had included three of Malaysia's famous gardens comprising the Lake Gardens, Putrajaya Botanical Garden and Sabah Agriculture Park among the most enduring and beautiful gardens in Asia, has inspired us to promote our scenic gardens to the world.

We are also delighted to sponsor the Special Malaysia edition of the book as all book sales go towards the Chelsea Pensioner's Appeal Fund. The grounds of the Royal Hospital, home of the Chelsea Pensioners are also the home of the annual Chelsea Flower Show where Tourism Malaysia is exhibiting a Malaysian garden for the first time. It is therefore very appropriate indeed for us to support this unique book while at the same time helping one of the UK's most steadfast and time honoured charities.

I believe that there are some things that can only be expressed through illustrations and pictures; and the beauty of gardens and parks are one of them. I am hoping that the mesmeric photo collection in this art form coffee table book will entice garden enthusiasts from all over the world to come and visit our enchanting gardens and parks.

Thank you.

"MALAYSIA TRULY ASIA"

Tasik Melati, Perlis

Forest Research Institute Malaysia, Selangor

Taman Seribu Bunga, Melaka

Hibiscus Garden, Kuala Lumpur

Mount Kinabalu, Sabah

# Paradise Found

JOURNEYS THROUGH **NOBLE GARDENS OF ASIA**

THE CHELSEA
PENSIONERS'
*Appeal*

**BOOK COMMITTEE**

CHAIRMAN
SIR RONALD GRIERSON

MEMBERS
HH PRINCESS SORAYA DAKHLAH
JOAN FOO MAHONY
ROY RATAZZI CBE
SARAH TILLIE
PENNY WALKER
SARAH WILLIAMS

**PRODUCTION**

GENERAL EDITOR
HH PRINCESS SORAYA DAKHLAH

PHOTO EDITOR
NATASHA O'CONNOR

PROJECT ADMINISTRATOR
DEBORAH PEREIRA

DESIGN
IMAYA WONG, GRAINSTUDIO

PAPER SUPPLIER
FINE PAPER TAKEO (M) SDN. BHD.

COLOUR SEPARATION
UNICO SERVICES

MAPS
ANDREW RICE

CONCEPT BY
JOAN FOO MAHONY AND HH PRINCESS SORAYA DAKHLAH

First published in 2008 by
Cross Time Matrix Sdn. Bhd. (611448-A)
Suite 19.06A
19th Floor
Menara MAA
12 Jalan Dewan Bahasa
50460 Kuala Lumpur
Malaysia

Phone +60 3 2144 5333
Fax +60 3 2144 2331
Email contact@crosstimematrix.com

Cross Time Matrix is a leading boutique publisher of award winning coffee table books. Other titles from Cross Time Matrix include:

Mahathir: 22 Years, 22 Voices

Food From the Heart: Malaysia's Culinary Heritage (winner of the 2005 Gourmand World Cookbook Awards)

Straits Chinese Porcelain

From Yangon to Manila Bay: The Cruising Almanac 2005

PRINTED AND BOUND IN MALAYSIA BY
TIMES OFFSET (M) SDN. BHD.

**ISBN 9789833214037**

# CONTENTS

As I know from my own experience, the garden can become a glimpse of Paradise; a place of escape from the rush of the world where humanity, Nature and the Divine meet in harmony.

This beautiful book brings that glimpse of Paradise into our lives. As a retrospective of the most beautiful gardens of Asia, it enables the reader to appreciate the spiritual relationship between Nature, in all Her glory, and Man as the custodian of the gardens.

Yet this book is not only a practical guide to some of the most enchanting gardens of Asia, but a gesture of kindness towards a group of individuals in need. All the proceeds from Paradise Found will contribute towards the Chelsea Pensioners' Appeal in the United Kingdom and it is in this capacity, as Patron of the Appeal, and not only as a passionate gardener, that I write this message.

The Chelsea Pensioners, some of Britain's true war heroes and veterans from past campaigns, live in the Royal Hospital Chelsea - itself one of the world's most splendid buildings, the grounds of which host the famous Chelsea Flower Show. The Appeal hopes to raise £35 million by 2008 for the improvement of the medical and residential facilities within the Royal Hospital so that, by purchasing this book, you have helped to benefit the lives of those to whom we owe the most. The Royal Hospital has achieved much over the last 300 years, but it is now time to look to the future.

I sincerely hope you will enjoy this fine book and that it will provide you with new and harmonious inspiration.

# MESSAGE FROM THE MARQUESS OF SALISBURY PC DL

CHAIRMAN OF THE APPEAL EXECUTIVE COMMITTEE

The Royal Hospital Chelsea is the home of the Chelsea Pensioners. These gentlemen in their scarlet coats are a familiar sight in and around Chelsea and are a British national institution. The Chelsea Pensioners live in one of the world's great buildings: conceived and designed by Sir Christopher Wren, with additions by his worthy successor in architectural greatness, Sir John Soane. The grounds of the Hospital are also the home of the annual Chelsea Flower Show, surely the world's finest horticultural event. The Chelsea Pensioner and horticulture are thus intimately connected in an extraordinary setting.

How appropriate, therefore, that this unique book should be about gardens. The money it raises will contribute to the Chelsea Pensioners' Appeal whose proceeds will pay for a new infirmary and for modernising the Long Wards where the pensioners live. Looking after those that have kept us safe in their old age seems to me the best of causes.

*Salisbury.*

# THE ROYAL HOSPITAL CHELSEA AND THE CHELSEA PENSIONERS' APPEAL

THE CHELSEA PENSIONERS' *Appeal*

The Royal Hospital Chelsea—the home of the Chelsea Pensioners—was founded by King Charles II in 1682 for 'the succour and relief of those broken by age or war'. For well over 300 years since then it has provided a fitting home and community for successive generations of veteran soldiers who have served their country faithfully and selflessly. It is a manifestation of the unwritten but essential contract that, in return for the sacrifice made by those in the Forces, the Nation will ensure they are equipped properly, given the best possible care if they become casualties, and treated fairly. Today it continues to do just this, looking after some 300 pensioners with an average age of 84. It is a living memorial to those who have given their lives, and a refuge to those in need who served their country and survived. The much loved figure of the Chelsea Pensioner is, in a sense, the visible expression of the unbreakable covenant between Nation, Government and Army.

Today the Royal Hospital Chelsea needs financial help. If it is to continue providing a fitting home and community for old and infirm soldiers it must modernise the facilities it offers. If it fails in this venture a small but significant part of the fabric of the Nation will wither and die. The first step is the building of a new infirmary that complies with modern care standards legislation, work on which is already well underway. This is where those who are nearing the end of their lives, and those in need of full-time care, are looked after with great dignity until they die.

But the Infirmary is only part of the overall modernisation programme. Much of the living accommodation in the old Christopher Wren buildings would still be recognised by the first intake of Chelsea Pensioners in 1692. It is primitive by modern standards and must now be brought into the 21st Century.

And because the Royal Hospital is one of London's greatest buildings, which is Grade 1 listed, this is a hugely challenging task, and an expensive one.

The basis of the Chelsea Pensioners' Appeal is simply this: if Britain, as a nation, is going to honour those who have served their country—if the Royal Hospital is going to deliver on its part of the covenant—£35 million must be found.

Some may consider this the task of the Government. However, this is not quite so straightforward and lies in historical practice—for even Stephen Fox, Charles II's Paymaster General, had to raise the money privately when the hospital was built.

The Government has continued to grant us our annual running costs since we were founded, but in recent years these have become very much subject to the vagaries of the public spending round. And we do cherish our independence. Our major capital projects after the war were funded by war reparations money and minor capital expenditure has been funded from the Royal Hospital's small investment portfolio. Our distant predecessors must have felt that this was how it should be, that there was no need to raise further funds and no attempt to establish an endowment was made. By comparison, our sister establishment for sailors, The Royal Hospital Greenwich, which closed as a veteran sailors home about 150 years ago, did establish an endowment, which today still exists as a grant-giving fund of over £200M. So, our whole development plan is geared to set up the beginnings of an endowment for our future.

Nowadays other factors have come to play, as charity and government can be indistinguishable, with ministers turning to the "voluntary sector" to plug the gap left by a dwindling welfare state. A gap for which, many of us would argue, the government has a clear responsibility. This at a time when the battle for donations is growing fiercer by the year with thousands of different charity voices fighting to be heard by a limited pool of donors.

The cause may not be as romantic or obvious as some others. Old people in society have been increasingly marginalised and are in danger of being isolated. For many people there arc other charities, notably those for children, which may appear more attractive. But while there are undoubtedly many worthy causes, the plight of a Nation's old soldiers must surely be second to none.

There is a quality about the Royal Hospital not shared by other institutions and which could not be replicated. For it is, in effect, a self-contained village centred on its own chapel, its communal dining hall, its infirmary and its social club. It is a community of old gentlemen, (and soon to be old ladies) with similar backgrounds and experiences. It has already survived criminal mismanagement and several attempts to close it down. In two world wars it suffered grievous damage and many casualties. Today it stands high in the affection and regard of the public and the famous scarlet coat has become a singular and exclusive badge of honour.

The In-Pensioners may seem to epitomise the old grandeur and greatness of our nation, but they are a present and constant link with the past, and the veterans of Mons and Alamein worship in the same chapel, sit at the same dining tables and take their ease in the same Colonnade as the ghosts of Ramillies and Fontenoy, of Plessey, Albuera and Inkerman. The battle honours inscribed on the panels of the Great Hall tell the enduring story of the British Army: but the old soldiers are themselves the living embodiment of that story. This sense of continuity informs and underlies the special and unique quality of Chelsea.

The Royal Hospital is unusual in another sense. It is neither a barracks nor an old peoples' home. The In-Pensioners are neither serving soldiers nor retired civilians. Here, in their village setting, the old soldiers enjoy privacy and peace in their twilight years and a dignity in death, to which they are entitled. It is also a village in which the age of chivalry is by no means dead.

The plea is thus to help The Royal Hospital to look after the Chelsea Pensioners of today—and even more so, those of tomorrow. Whatever you can do will be much appreciated.

# FINDING PARADISE IN PARADISE FOUND

Which is the most beautiful garden in the World?

—or... the oldest
the largest
the boldest
the most expensive...

Beauty is in the eye of the beholder, so my favourite garden may well not be yours, as we each see different facets of its beauty, as in a diamond with many faces. The other factor which determines our choices is that we can only judge those we have seen, possibly leaving numerous gems out of our experience.

*Paradise Found* allows us to get at least a taste of many people's choices throughout Asia—the birthplace of gorgeous gardens. It allows us into secret places and glimpses of paradise over a continent so large that few of us could possibly explore them all in reality. From the symmetry of the Mughal Gardens in Pakistan and India through the lush tropical feast of South East Asia to the sculpted symbolism ever present in the gardens of China and Japan, we are taken on a rich journey through the relationship between history and garden design throughout the mystical East.

As we turn the pages we are drawn from one outstandingly beautiful environment to the next, every garden having its own story to tell, its own personality to appreciate, together with an individual character—created by its designer.

We in the West owe so much to the traditions, style and philosophy of Asian gardens. I believe that we tend to take our gardens too superficially, missing the deeper qualities found in so many gardens of the Orient.

As an English garden designer, I have been greatly influenced in my profession from my experiences working with Asian designers, whose ideas have made me reflect on how I can make my designs more meaningful and complete. I always start with the dream—however outlandish it may be. Certainly practicality has to come in—never to overrule the vision, but to provide the means to make it work. I have been involved in a number of outstanding Japanese Gardens in England, with master designer Koji Ninomiya bringing the Japanese influence to a Western environment with his symbolic use of rocks, water and bamboo forests.

A garden is more than just a place of beauty—it has to become an experience of peace and tranquillity, where a person can be totally absorbed by the whole environment. And it is the creator of each garden who lends himself inherently and immortally to that garden. From the ancient gardens of the region through to the more contemporary gardens like the Rock Garden of Chandigarh or Nong Nooch in Thailand, the mark and imprint of the creator is ever present.

In every culture, styles can vary considerably—there is no such thing as a "typical" Chinese, Japanese, Indian or even English Garden. From the formal to the informal; the grand to the cottage garden; the public to the private—each space must be carefully assessed by the designer, ensuring that the garden meets the needs of those it serves, and complements or enhances the whole environment. Regardless of style, culture or climate the sentiments are the same, to rejoice in nature.

Each garden in this book has its own personality, with its strengths and weaknesses. Our experience in one may be a sense of awe, in others serenity, grandeur, simplicity, history, horticultural excellence and many more ways that uplift our souls. If a garden does not uplift and inspire it is missing its *raison d'être*.

I believe that the most important ingredient in any garden, be it large or small, is... Atmosphere: it has to be a place where we feel good without necessarily knowing why, and where we can feast our eyes as well as our souls. Here we can experience the hand of God and the hand of man working in partnership to make at least a small part of the World into a slice of paradise. As a designer this can be achieved in a variety of ways and through the use of the elements, not just in terms of vegetation but through water, through rock and stone, through light and air.

Garden design is a fascinating marriage between nature and architecture, drawing these two disciplines together in a unique way. There are those which are heavily structured, where plants are decorative additions, whilst at the other extreme, there are gardens which are so natural it is hard to spot the hand of man.

Each has its place; each has a contribution to making the World a better and more beautiful place.

There is so much ugliness around us, mostly man made, that we must rejoice that gardens are shining examples of how we can create and enjoy that which is truly beautiful and good. I pray for the day when instead of war and destruction, we can turn our gifts and skills towards making our world even more beautiful, providing everyone the opportunity to breathe clean air and to relax and appreciate the garden.

*Paradise Found* weaves a rich tapestry of such beauty throughout Asia, allowing us all to appreciate how different cultures and generations interpret the word: **"GARDEN"**.

**JULIAN DOWLE**
LANDSCAPE ARCHITECT
GLOUCESTERSHIRE, UNITED KINGDOM

Soswaewon Garden, Jeollonam-do, Republic of Korea. JEAN CHUNG

Jahangir's Tomb Garden, Lahore, Pakistan. WARRICK PAGE / PANOS PICTURES

Shalimar Bagh, Lahore, Pakistan.
WARRICK PAGE / PANOS PICTURES

# SOUTH ASIA

PAKISTAN   INDIA   SRI LANKA

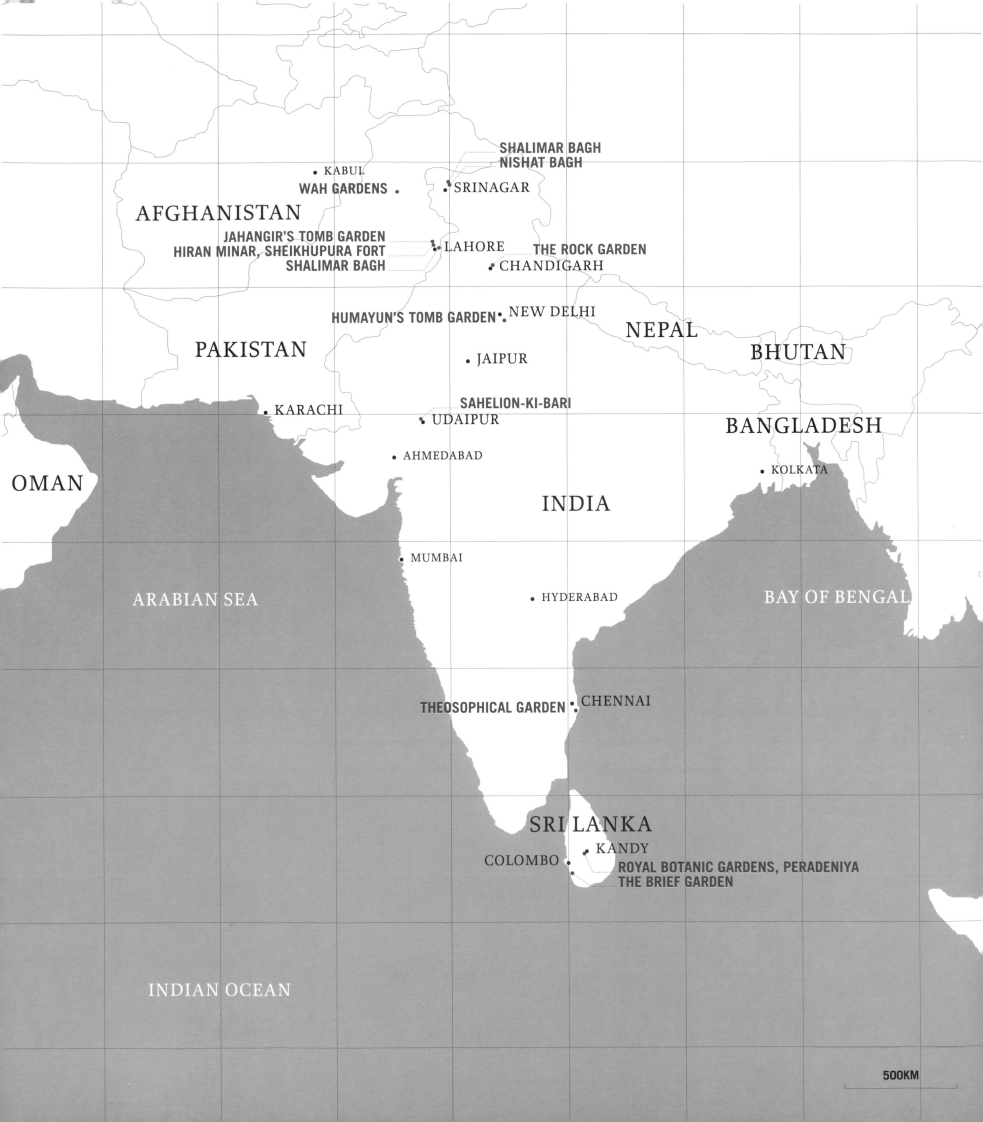

KABUL

SHALIMAR BAGH
NISHAT BAGH

WAH GARDENS

SRINAGAR

AFGHANISTAN

JAHANGIR'S TOMB GARDEN
HIRAN MINAR, SHEIKHUPURA FORT
SHALIMAR BAGH

LAHORE

THE ROCK GARDEN

CHANDIGARH

HUMAYUN'S TOMB GARDEN

NEW DELHI

NEPAL

BHUTAN

PAKISTAN

JAIPUR

KARACHI

SAHELION-KI-BARI

UDAIPUR

BANGLADESH

AHMEDABAD

OMAN

KOLKATA

INDIA

MUMBAI

ARABIAN SEA

HYDERABAD

BAY OF BENGAL

THEOSOPHICAL GARDEN

CHENNAI

SRI LANKA

KANDY

COLOMBO

ROYAL BOTANIC GARDENS, PERADENIYA
THE BRIEF GARDEN

INDIAN OCEAN

500KM

# THE GARDENS OF SOUTH ASIA: ANCIENT TO MODERN

The twelve remarkable and noble gardens from India, Pakistan and Sri Lanka illustrated in this chapter vividly express the rich stylistic diversity and creativity found in the design of gardens in South Asia. Four core concepts or themes were fundamental to the development and creation of these gardens which drew inspiration from a complex history that stretches back in time nearly three thousand years. These were patronage, power, paradise and pleasure.

Simply stated, noble gardens require noble patrons. Social backgrounds, motivations and resources may vary greatly, but a common will and resolve to create a garden which can often rise to the status of a great work of art, however transitory, connect the humble householder and merchant, temple priest and saint, architect and artisan, minister and maharajah and up to the emperor himself.

Many of the grandest gardens in South Asia were built by invaders from outside and conquerors from within. The establishment and recognition of their power was crucial to the success of the state. The very act of creating gardens which could harness the rivers and streams, bring beauty to the barren wilderness and provide sustenance for the population was a potent political statement not only of the rulers' ability to control nature but that they were also here to stay.

The sacred geographies and cosmologies of the ancient world shared many common creation myths, heroic epics, folk tales and legends. The concept of the lush paradise garden surrounded by walls and divided into sections by free-flowing water channels originated in ancient Sumer and Mesopotamia in the second and third millennium BC. In South Asia, veneration of the sacred mountain and temple groves where the Tree of Knowledge grew were basic to the three great faiths of Hinduism, Jainism and Buddhism which took root here. An early Sanskrit text somehow seemed to know that 'the gods always play where groves are, near rivers, mountains and in towns with pleasure gardens'.

Pleasure, both personal and public, must be one of the central motivations in the creation of any garden. In South Asia, this was raised to an art form. Extraordinary pavilions of pleasure surrounded by tranquil pools and the sound of running water were adorned with carved marble screens, glittering mirror-work, glazed tiles and wall paintings which added to the other worldly quality found in many gardens. They became idyllic retreats where days and nights could be spent in meditation, recreation, entertainment and experiencing the sheer pleasure of nature.

Although very little remains of early gardens in South Asia, we know from the Sanskrit poetry of Kalidasa and other classical writers that beautiful gardens were created in the imperial Mauryan and Gupta capitals of Pataliputra from the fourth century BC to the sixth century AD. The taming of the land and the establishment of cultivated gardens and parks were associated from the very beginning with the role of the kind and giving benevolent ruler, the Chakravartin.

To be an educated and cultured member of society, gardening was one of the sixty-four arts to be perfected. The *Kamasutra*, guided its readers through many esoteric aspects of life including the importance of maintaining gardens: 'He is indeed a monarch if his house has extensive and spacious gardens containing large pools of water with lovely lotus blossoms over which humming bees fly. This may be regarded as the consummation of all happiness.' One of the many Sanskrit words for flower, *sumansa*, means 'that which pleasures the mind'. A variety of techniques and systems of horticulture and water harvesting were practiced while plants and trees were also systematically studied in order to understand their medicinal and commercial properties.

With the collapse of the Gupta Empire in the mid-sixth century, a number of regional Hindu kingdoms emerged across the subcontinent. Some of the most powerful and wealthy states were established in Rajasthan by Rajput rulers, hereditary clans of warriors, who traced their dynastic origins back to the sun, moon and fire. Tempted by the fabled riches of Hindu temples and the overflowing treasuries of the maharajahs, the Afghan conqueror, Muhammad Ghori, invaded India in 1192 and defeated the great Rajput king Prithviraj Chauhan at the battle of Tarain near Delhi. This momentous battle ushered in a period of centralised Muslim rule in much of north and central India under a series of dynasties known collectively as the Delhi Sultanate which maintained varying degrees of centralised control for the next four hundred years. Recent archaeological excavations, the study of miniatures and medieval texts reveal that the tradition of creating gardens in temples, palaces and towns continued to flourish throughout this long period, but it is not until the arrival of the Mughals in the early sixteenth century that our knowledge of South Asian gardens stands on firmer ground.

Babur, the first Mughal emperor, traced his impressive lineage back to Genghis Khan and Timur. In search of even greater glory, he left Ferghana, his ancestral kingdom in Central Asia, and invaded India in 1526 defeating Sultan Ibrahim Lodi at the historic battle of Panipat. During his short reign of only four years, Babur laid the foundation for a vast and powerful empire that would change the political, social and cultural face of South Asia for centuries.

Although they were to build some of the most magnificent cities, palaces, bazaars, mosques, gardens and tombs the world had ever seen, the Mughals never forgot their nomadic roots which instilled in them a deep respect and fascination with the natural world. In his exceptionally frank and lively memoirs, the *Baburnama* written in Chaghatay Turkish, Babur deplored the poor gardens he discovered in India which he thought lacked symmetry and pleasing water features. Between conquests and consolidation of the new empire, he set about to change that. On the bank of the Yamuna River in Agra, he erected the Garden of Eight Paradises, a walled garden designed in traditional Timurid *chahar bagh* style which was partitioned into four or more sections and cooled by flowing water channels. Although little remains of this important early pleasure garden, it started a trend of building riverside gardens in Delhi and Agra by members of the Imperial family and Mughal nobility which carried on well into the eighteenth century.

The first major Mughal building complex incorporated within a formal garden was the imposing tomb of Babur's son, Humayun, completed in 1571 in Delhi. The style is late Timurid but the materials and superb craftsmanship are entirely indigenous. Rajasthani quarries supplied the red sandstone and white marble which were used to clad the building, and master stone carvers fashioned the pierced geometric screens which allowed a dappled light to fall onto the solitary tomb of the emperor. Persian water wheels operated by teams of bullocks raised the water to storage tanks from where it tumbled down carved sandstone chutes into the pools and sunken channels of the main garden. The ancient imagery of paradise recreated on an earthly plane was now firmly established as an integral part of Mughal garden design and on a monumental scale previously unseen.

Akbar continued his father's legacy with the construction of Fatehpur Sikr, majestic new fortified city built in celebration of his conquest of Gujarat. Formal gardens, pavilions of pleasure and pools of water were major features inside the private quarters of the palace. He also maintained mini-palaces, caravanserais and halting places for the Imperial family, ministers, itinerant merchants and troops as they moved from one end of the rapidly expanding empire to the other. The locations were often selected for their natural beauty next to lakes or streams where palatial lodges surrounded by formal gardens would be constructed. The legend goes that the Wah Gardens near Peshawar was so extraordinary that Akbar uttered the Persian exclamation, 'wah' or 'wow', when he first encountered the site.

The Mughals were passionate hunters and Akbar's heir, Jahangir, was the most enthusiastic of them all. His elegant octagonal hunting lodge at Sheikhupura, was strategically placed in the middle of an artificial tank surrounded by groves of trees and gardens. Jahangir was also a keen naturalist and he encouraged the court artists to record the beauties as well as the oddities of the plant and animal world. In 1620, entranced by his visit to Kashmir which became the summer capital of the Mughals, he commissioned a number of gardens including one of the most exquisite of all pleasure gardens, the Farah Bakhsh or Joy-Imparting Garden built on the lower terrace at Shalimar. Continuing the tradition established by his father, Jahangir's majestic tomb in Lahore was placed in the middle of a formal garden and displays very fine stone carving and inlay work.

Shah Jahan, the King of the World, inherited the Mughal throne from Jahangir and became the greatest builder of them all. He expanded the original Shalimar Gardens in Kashmir and founded a new garden of the same name in Lahore. His father-in-law, Yamin al-Daula Asaf Khan, a leading member of the Mughal nobility, commissioned the glorious Nishat Bagh or Garden of Gladness on the bank of the Dal Lake in Kashmir as well.

Shah Jahan is perhaps best remembered for the Taj Mahal, an architectural masterpiece which brought the concept of the Mughal tomb garden to its sublime conclusion. In 1639, Shah Jahan decided to move the Mughal capital from Agra to Delhi, and over the next ten years, he oversaw the construction of the resplendent city of Shahjahanabad on the bank of the Yamuna River. Inside the massive Red Fort, a series of white marble palaces cooled by lotus-shaped pools and water channels led onto elegant formal gardens. On the polished walls of the Hall of Private Audience, a Persian verse in gilded letters reads: 'If there is a paradise on earth, it is here, it is here, it is here'

After a violent succession struggle, Shah Jahan's son, Aurangzeb, ascended to the throne. He was the last Mughal emperor with any real power and he spent most of the forty-nine years of his long reign trying to hold the vast empire together until his death in 1707. As Mughal power and cultural influence gradually ebbed away in the eighteenth century, new developments in painting, architecture and garden design based on local traditions and styles began to flourish in a number of provincial kingdoms which were experiencing something of a renaissance. In Udaipur, the legendary city of lakes, the charming Sahelion-ki-Bari Garden built by the maharajah for the enjoyment of his queen and the ladies of the court exhibits late Mewari style at its whimsical best.

Colonial powers were at the same time competing for control of the 'jewel in the crown'. After a long struggle which pitted local rulers against each other, the British prevailed, and in 1857 the last Mughal emperor, Bahadur Shah Zafar was banished to Rangoon never to return. Under the central direction of Kew Gardens in London, botanical gardens were set up across the length and breadth of the empire. Renowned for its avenue of royal palms, the Royal Botanic Gardens in Peradeniya, perpetuate the ancient practice of combining great natural beauty with important research into the nature and property of plants.

India has for millennia attracted dedicated seekers of esoteric knowledge and spiritual enlightenment. The Theosophical Garden in Chennai, shaded by one of the largest banyan trees in Asia, was cultivated as a retreat for meditation, reflection and healing, recalling the sacred groves and temple gardens of the classical Buddhist and Hindu periods.

When the British moved their capital from Calcutta to Delhi in 1911, the design of the new city and magnificent government buildings developed by Edwin Lutyens and Herbert Baker incorporated many elements drawn from the rich heritage of secular and sacred architecture from all parts of the subcontinent. The Viceroy's Palace, at the centre of New Delhi, was not considered complete without a grand Mughal Garden symbolically demonstrating, as it had so many times before, that the empire was here to stay.

In the second half of the twentieth century, independence brought a new spirit of individual creativity to garden design in South Asia unfettered by imperial or regional styles. The exquisite Brief Garden, designed by Bevis Bawa, around his Sri Lankan home, and Nek Chand's enchanting Rock Garden in Chandigarh combine art, nature and water features in imaginative new directions while at the same time embracing indigenous materials and building techniques.

There are encouraging signs that across South Asia the ancient tradition of creating noble gardens is alive and well. In Jaipur, the capital of Rajasthan, a long-abandoned eighteenth-century water palace, the Jal Mahal, has been recently restored to its earlier splendour. On the roof-top terrace, a new garden, the Chameli Bagh or Jasmine Garden, nears completion inspired by the designs of earlier Mughal and Rajput gardens. Master sandstone and marble carvers and traditional artists work side by side with a team of engineers, experts in lighting and water technology, horticulturists and naturalists. Even in the twenty-first century, paradise can still be found.

**MITCHELL ABDUL KARIM CRITES**
ART AND ARCHITECTURE HISTORIAN, SARAY FOUNDER
JAIPUR, INDIA

# WAH GARDENS
## WAH, PUNJAB PAKISTAN

WAH WAS ONE OF THE MAJOR CAMPSITES OF THE MUGHAL TRAVELLING THROUGH THE REGION AND A FAVOURED SPOT OF MANY MUGHAL RULERS. THE GARDENS WERE FED BY WATER THAT COLLECTED IN A TANK ON THE UPPER TERRACE WHICH THEN FLOWED DOWN THROUGH A *BARADARI* AND TWO PAVILIONS, ONE OF WHICH HOUSED A MAGNIFICENT HAMMAM OR BATHING ROOM. THE GARDENS THEMSELVES WERE PLANTED WITH TOWERING CYPRESS TREES WHICH LINED THE WATER CHANNELS AND PAVILIONS BUILT BY SUCCESSIVE MUGHAL EMPERORS. NOTABLY, WAH'S TRANSFORMATION FROM A SIMPLE RETREAT TO ONE OF IMPERIAL PROPORTIONS CAN BE ATTRIBUTED TO RAJA MAN SINGH, THE BROTHER-IN-LAW OF JAHANGIR. IN 1980 THE GARDENS WERE DECLARED A WORLD HERITAGE SITE BY UNESCO AND TODAY THE GARDENS ARE SLOWLY BEING RESTORED TO THEIR ORIGINAL BEAUTY.

Off the Grand Trunk Road from Lahore to Peshawar, just after the ancient Buddhist ruins of Taxila, is a remarkable 16-17th century Mughal garden. Fed by natural springs, Wah was a favourite *manzil gah* or halting place for the Mughals during their journeys to and from Kabul.

No one knows how it came by its name but legend has it that the Emperor Akbar, on seeing this verdant spot, exclaimed: "Wah!" (Wonderful!). Early accounts don't refer to it as a garden and Wah lacks the precise symmetry of other Mughal gardens, perhaps because it was simply a scenic spot that was developed into a formal garden over a long period.

Akbar passed through several times and the Rajput Hindu noble Man Singh, who was his governor of Kabul from 1585-1587, built a small pavilion in the middle of a basin. Jahangir visited Wah six times between 1607 and 1626 and has left a delightful account of the garden. In his memoirs he mentions a waterfall, which is no longer there, but which he claims was the only one of its kind on the way to Kabul. "I halted three days at this enchanting place," he says, "drinking wine with those who were intimate with me and... catching fish." Having caught twelve, he put pearls in their noses and threw them back in the water.

The site also appealed to Shah Jahan who ordered improvements: much of its appearance today is credited to his period. There are numerous contemporary references to the garden with his chroniclers referring to it glowingly as *Bagh-e-Bahisht 'Ain* (Vision of Paradise) and comparing it with the legendary Garden of Irum.

After the fall of the Mughals, the garden was vandalized and fell into neglect. In 1865 it was granted by the British to Mohammad Hayat Khan, ADC to Gen. John Nicholson. It was taken back by the Government in 1976 and some excavation and restoration work has been done.

The crumbling shell of the *baradari* (summer house) still has traces of the fine stucco work which must have embellished its interior. Each of its wings had a verandah from which the ladies of the *zenana* may have looked across the shimmering waters of the tank to the *mahtabi* (moonlight pavilion) where the king and his courtiers enjoyed the pleasures of the night.

Twenty-two magnificent cypress trees stand like sentinels on the edges of the central water channel in the lower terrace and the garden is dotted with a variety of fruit trees, including *jamun (Eugenia jambolana)*, mango, loquat, plum, apricot and white mulberry. But in winter the garden looks stark: a cold wind comes down from the mountains and the *chinar (Platanus orientalis)* are bereft of leaves. The trunks of a couple have been hollowed out by mischievous boys throwing lighted tapers to get at the parrots' nests inside. More alarming, however, is the damp around the reservoir. The walls need to be checked for leakages and reinforced; otherwise this extraordinary garden, which quickened the footsteps of kings, may be tragically and irredeemably lost.

**DURDANA SOOMRO**
AUTHOR
KARACHI, PAKISTAN

# JAHANGIR'S TOMB GARDEN
## LAHORE, PUNJAB PAKISTAN

THIS TOMB GARDEN OF THE 4TH MUGHAL EMPEROR, JAHANGIR (REIGN 1605-1627) WAS COMMISSIONED BY HIS SON SHAH JAHAN (REIGN 1628-1658) TEN YEARS AFTER HIS FATHER'S DEATH. JAHANGIR'S TOMB WAS BUILT ON THE SITE OF *BAGH-I DILKUSHA*, A GARDEN DESIGNED BY JAHANGIR'S WIFE, NUR JAHAN. THE EMPEROR JAHANGIR WAS NOTED FOR SOME OF THE MOST MAGNIFICENT AND BEGUILING GARDENS IN INDIA AND PAKISTAN INCLUDING SHALIMAR BAGH IN KASHMIR AND HIRAN MINAR IN LAHORE. THE TOMB ITSELF RISES FROM A PODIUM, WHILE THE RECTANGULAR GARDEN IS DISSECTED INTO FOUR BY WATER CHANNELS. FOUNTAINS ORIGINALLY SPRANG FROM THE POOLS SURROUNDING THE TOMB AND CASCADING WATER ADDED TO THE MESMERISING EFFECT.

In November 1627 AD, a Mughal retinue carried the body of Nuruddin Jahangir Padshah, fourth ruler of the Mughal empire that spanned South Asia in the 16th through 18th centuries, from the mountain town of Rajaur where he reportedly died with the word "Kashmir" on his lips. A shrine on the road from Kashmir at Bhimbar marks the site of his funeral and purported burial place of his intestines. The funeral procession continued east along the Grand Trunk Road, the ancient highway from Kabul to Kolkata, perhaps halting at Jahangir's former princely estate at Sheikhupura with its magnificent Hiran Minar water complex where he buried his beloved pet antelope that helped him hunt other animals (one of the many contradictions that Jahangir describes in his memoirs). They crossed Mughal brick bridges, masonry fragments of which still survive, halting on the Ravi riverbank opposite the citadel of Lahore.

Outside the city limits, in accordance with Islamic law, a pleasure garden was re-configured to become Jahangir's tomb-garden. The area became a royal funerary complex that also included the tomb-gardens for Jahangir's powerful queen Nur Jahan (d. 1645) and her brother Asaf Khan (d. 1641). These gardens are linked by an entry court known as the Akbari Serai, which provided the preferred southern entry for Jahangir's tomb. The area is known as Shahdara, which may have meant the "king's gateway," to and from Lahore—the Mughal city of gardens.

Today one approaches Jahangir's tomb-garden from the opposite direction, in modern ways that can obscure the garden experience. Imagine driving through a metropolis of 8 million people at high speed or in a bumper-to-bumper crawl along urban highways that skirt the Mughal citadel with high fortress-gardens built by Jahangir and his successors. On a clear day, the tomb-garden minarets across the river are visible from the ramparts. Today, one crosses a wide stretch of developed floodplain created by the westward migration of the river and city, toward a highway bridge that replaced the Mughal bridge-of-boats and ferry.

To envision the riverfront landscape in Mughal times, I always take a sharp turn off the road just before the bridge, down to the riverbank, and row out to an island garden known as Kamran's Baradari, reportedly built by Jahangir's rebellious grand-uncle Mirza Kamran in the 1630s, which would have made it the oldest Mughal garden in Lahore. The island is covered with wild grasses, gnarled trees, and sand from floods that cut it off from the Shahdara riverbank and eroded its edges and structures. The rushing river muted traffic and city, allowing leisurely explorations of the garden complex and its half-ruined pavilion set within a water tank, connected to an upper garden terrace ornamented with a unique star-shaped pool. In 1990 the garden was re-constructed with modern materials: the *baradari* was rebuilt, plastered, and painted; new fountains and lights installed, the star-shaped pool filled; the garden turfed and made accessible to motor-boats, paddle boats, and jet skis.

We interviewed visitors to Kamran's Baradari before and after reconstruction and learned many interesting things, for example, that a legendary tunnel ran beneath the river, and that when Lahoris thought of paradise-like places men tended to think of Aurangzeb's Badshahi mosque while women tended to think of the shrine *(dargah)* of the famous 11th century Sufi saint al-Hujwiri or more affectionately Data Ganj Baksh ("Bestower of Treasures"). Those who enjoyed Kamran's Baradari before reconstruction shifted to the place that came closest to what they called its historical and peaceful "feeling" —Jahangir's tomb-garden in Shahdara.

This detour to Kamran's Baradari always prepares me to approach Jahangir's tomb-garden in fresh ways: to explore its location and surroundings along the Ravi River flood terrace; to appreciate its progression through forecourts and thresholds before entering the garden; to look closely at its landscape as the Mughals did; and to experience its serenity even among the occasional busload of friendly school children.

What is this "feeling"? Imagine your first view of the garden seen from its monumental gateway: your eyes sweep across a panoramic square enclosure 600 Mughal yards wide and focus on a central brick-lined water channel exactly 1 Mughal yard wide. Measured drawings reveal that every structural element in the garden is decimally proportioned: 1, 5, 10, 20, 50, 100 yards, etc. One perceives, feels, this progression in scale from the monumental to the intimate. Then imagine Jahangir's tomb, a single-storey square red sandstone and tile-decorated structure that stands on a plinth with towering minarets at each corner. Architectural historians have commented on this "empty space" between its minarets where other Mughal tombs have either upper storeys or a dome and have offered various explanations. Experientially, the emptiness is palpable. Finally, imagine the garden vegetation within this powerful architectural and landscape space. The central axis of pruned shrubs, manicured turf, and potted annuals has a late-colonial, now post-colonial style; but it gives way to looser vegetation in the outer garden quadrants. In a few wonderful places, the large clumps of trees that flank garden walkways include tough palms and tall *jamun* trees that bear a purple fruit, as well as whatever droughts and floods the fierce Punjab summers can deliver. In these areas modern landscaping reverts to the "domesticated wild" character observable in the landscape backdrops of many Mughal paintings.

Jahangir's tomb-garden in Lahore thus retains some key elements of the form, feeling, and meanings associated with Mughal gardens. Although presently diminished at the other Shahdara tomb-gardens of Asaf Khan, Nur Jahan, and Kamran's Baradari, fragments of these elements can still be discerned, and will hopefully be cultivated through conservation for future generations in the Mughal City of Gardens.

**PROFESSOR JAMES L. WESCOAT JR**
PROFESSOR & HEAD OF THE DEPARTMENT OF LANDSCAPE ARCHITECTURE
UNIVERSITY OF ILLINOIS AT URBANA-CHAMPAIGN, UNITED STATES OF AMERICA

# HIRAN MINAR, SHEIKHUPURA FORT

SHEIKHUPURA, PUNJAB  PAKISTAN

THE EMPEROR JAHANGIR (REIGN 1605-1627), AS A YOUNG PRINCE, OFTEN ENJOYED HUNTING IN THE AREA KNOWN AS SHEIKHUPURA. IT WAS HIS NICKNAME THAT GIVES THE CURRENT LOCATION ITS NAME AND IT WAS HERE, AFTER SOME TIME, THAT HE BUILT A HUNTING LODGE FOR HIMSELF NEAR THE ARTIFICIAL LAKE. THE PRINCES GARDEN OR HIRAN MINAR IS SO-CALLED BECAUSE OF THE MINARET BUILT HERE IN HONOUR OF THE EMPEROR'S PET ANTELOPE, MANSRAJ. WITHIN THE GROUNDS ARE THE REMAINS OF JAHANGIR'S PALACE, DECORATED WITH PAINTINGS AND FRESCOES, AND THE SHEIKHUPURA FORT. IN HIS DIARY, JAHANGIR WROTE OF THE EVENTS IN 1607: "ON THE DAY OF TUESDAY, I RESIDE IN JAHANGIRPURA, MY HUNTING GROUND. ACCORDING TO MY ORDER, A MINAR AND A GRAVE FOR MY DEER, MANSRAJ, WERE CONSTRUCTED HERE."

Thirty eight kilometres from Lahore, in the vicinity of Sheikhupura, lies Hiran Minar, the celebrated hunting water-palace of Emperor Jahangir *(d. 1627)* built in memory of his favourite *hiran* (antelope) Mansraj.

Jahangirpur, as the emperor calls Sheikhupura in his memoirs *Tuzuk-i-Jahangiri*, was declared his "fixed hunting place," and the water-garden palace remained an important destination for the Mughals *en route* to Kashmir.

Jahangir had been gifted a "large and prosperous empire" conquered and consolidated by his father. His riches and wealth were legendary. It was not surprising then, that rather than the din of war, Jahangir enjoyed the pleasurable pursuits of feasts and entertainments, revelling in the company of poets and singers, writers and artists. His patronage of the arts was due mainly to the generally peaceful conditions but also to his own indolent temperament.

In his autobiography, Jahangir frequently records his delight in the spectacular *chahar bagh* (four-parterres) gardens that had been created by his ancestors—from Babur to Akbar—to spawn an introverted paradisal world in a dusty Hindustan, modelled with water channels, parterres, fountains and ponds. His obvious gratification in being close to nature, camping near streams and water reservoirs when on the march, is evident in his memoirs.

Hunting was a passionate pastime for all Mughal emperors and Jahangir was proud of his hunting prowess. When marching from Ajmer to Mandu in 1616, he confided his passion in his diary, "no day passed that I did not hunt while halting or travelling". On such expeditions, special arrangements were made in advance to allow the emperor to indulge in this lively sport and the number of animals captured and killed would be recorded in his *Tuzuk*.

Architecture was important to Jahangir for its enjoyment rather than as a symbol of power. Before his marriage in 1611 to the refined and cultured Mehr-un-Nisa, herself of Iranian descent, the future empress Nur Jahan, only a handful of buildings were built by Jahangir, the Hiran Minar among them. It was she who later became the force behind some of the magnificent buildings and superb paradisal gardens built during his reign. Where the original *manar* (tower) was built by Jahangir (1607), it can be safely conjectured that the unified concept of a formal planned water-garden ensemble with its handsome octagonal *baradari*—the *Daulat Khana* or palace residence—placed at the focal point of the *manar* in the middle of an enormous artificial water reservoir, was due to Nur Jahan.

Although greatly ravaged as a result of neglect over the past five hundred years, the breathtaking scale of the impressive assembly continues to overawe the visitor. It is not only the few remarkable structures but also the sheer scale of the ensemble and the enormous sprawling grounds extraordinary in their conception.

The original element of the Hiran Minar is the brick masonry *manar* (tower). From the base of a 33-foot wide octagon, battering upwards to a 22-foot diameter circular form, the robust brick masonry structure rises to 103 feet, towering above the countryside with its majestic height. The simple form of this five-stage spectacular tower is punctured with over 200 small apertures in 14 regular rows throughout the height, variously thought to have been used for anchoring hunting trophies in the Mughal tradition, or nesting of birds. An internal staircase, accessed through a narrow arched doorway, leads to the top, providing an extraordinary view from different stages of the tower of the surrounding countryside and its unlimited expanse.

Placed at the beginning of the causeway, the tower's ground floor panels are likely to have been beautified with decorative arabesques and patterns in fresco for the enjoyment of the royal party. The extant portion of a brick arcuate structure surrounding the lower part of the octagonal portion indicates existence of an encircling verandah.

At the base of the *manar* once lay the remains of Jahangir's favourite antelope Mansraj or Man Raj (my antelope), which the emperor acclaimed "was without equal in fights with tame antelopes and in hunting wild ones." The "gravestone in the shape of an antelope" mentioned by him is no longer extant, nor the couplets inscribed on the grave.

The royal retinue would arrive at the ceremonial pointed arch gateway. The gateway marks the edge of the enormous *hauz* or tank, traversed through a 308-foot long causeway supported on 21 brick masonry cusped-arch vaults. Treading or riding above the cool expanse of water the royal cavalcade would arrive at the palace building—the *daulat khana*—a brilliantly conceived elegant *hasht-bihisht* (eight sided) structure surmounted by a graceful *chattri* (cupola) casting its tremulous reflections in the clear waters of the reservoir. At night, the twinkling oil lamps lining the causeway and the palace apertures would create a charmed fairytale spectacle with their luminous multiple mirrored images—the whole ensemble brought to life in an area which was, at the time, a wilderness at best.

The *daulat khana* is the most refined structure of the ensemble. Decorated and outfitted as a royal residence, it is placed in the middle of the reservoir on a projecting octagonal platform in the tradition of Mughal *chahar bagh* sepulchres. The central octagonal chamber of the palace building rises to a full two-storey height, each side sporting lancet arched half-vaults. A small internal staircase provides access to upper-level apartments overlooking the central chamber through cusped-arch openings. On the first floor, each side of the octagonal palace building provides views through an arcuate *seh-dara*—an ensemble of three openings. From the remnants of decorative features, and in view of an inclination for strikingly ornamented surfaces in post-Akbar period, the interior would have been adorned with arabesques and medallions in finely executed fresco.

Kiosk pavilions stand guard as sentinels marking the four corners of the enormous reservoir and would also have been treated with fresco decoration similar to the *daulat khana*.

The *hauz*, in an unusual deference to the need of drinking water for animals, accommodates 65-foot wide brick-lined ramps, executed in herringbone pattern, on all its four sides that slope down to the water.

The magnificent water-garden palace of yesteryears is in a sad state of preservation, waiting to be restored to its former glory.

**YASMEEN LARI, *S.I.***
FOUNDER, LARI & ASSOCIATES
KARACHI, PAKISTAN

# SHALIMAR BAGH

## LAHORE, PUNJAB PAKISTAN

INSPIRED BY HIS FATHER'S GARDEN OF THE SAME NAME IN KASHMIR, SHALIMAR BAGH IS A 17TH CENTURY MUGHAL PLEASURE GARDEN, AND WAS LAID OUT BETWEEN 1637 AND 1642 FOR EMPEROR SHAH JAHAN (REIGN 1628-1658). BUILT BY ROYAL ARCHITECT AND ENGINEER, ALI MARDAN KAHAN WHO LATER BECAME A GOVERNOR OF KASHMIR, THIS UNESCO WORLD HERITAGE SITE IS MEANT TO BE A REPLICA OF THE ISLAMIC PARADISE. ENCASED IN HIGH FRET WORKED WALLS, THE GARDEN IS BASED ON THE PERSIAN STYLE OF *CHAHAR BAGH*, AND CONSISTS OF THREE ELEVATED TERRACES WITH PAVILIONS BUILT ON THREE SIDES. FLOWING THROUGH THE LEVELLED TERRACES IS THE ROYAL CANAL WHICH LEADS FROM THE RIVER AND FEEDS AN ASTOUNDING FOUR HUNDRED AND TEN WATER FOUNTAINS. THE GARDENS THEMSELVES ARE ABUNDANT WITH ODORIFEROUS TREES SUCH AS MANGO, ALMOND AND MULBERRY. WITH ITS HISTORY AND SPLENDOUR IT IS NO SURPRISE THAT THIS JEWEL OF LAHORE HAS ALWAYS HELD THE ROLE OF HOST TO THE GARDEN CITY'S FESTIVALS AND NATIONAL EVENTS.

An account of the life of the first Mughal Emperor Babur who lived in the sixteenth century, describes in poignant detail, the creation of a garden in his capital Kabul in Afghanistan. The *Bagh-e-Babur*, as it came to be known, became a model for subsequent Mughal Emperors who ruled India from the sixteenth century onwards for over 300 years. Though laid to waste during the recent civil conflict in Afghanistan, the *Bagh-e-Babur* has now been restored to its original form and represents the inspiration for a chain of Mughal gardens, including the Shalimar Gardens in Lahore, commenced by the Emperor Shah Jahan in 1637. Such gardens were designed to enhance the quality of the environment, to ornament the landscape, to provide recreation and repose, and to symbolize cultural and religious values and aspirations. As such, they are, together with architecture and the arts, among the most significant and enduring of Muslim expressions of the role and relationship of nature in its broader sense to human beings. Moreover gardens and landscape architecture in Muslim societies have been an important expression of ethical assumptions about stewardship, ecology, and the presence of beauty in the design of the built environment.

The Arabic word for garden (*jannah* translated into Persian and Urdu as *bagh*) is used in the Qur'an for paradise, the reward of the hereafter. One of the settings in the Qur'anic narrative of creation (Q 2:34, 7:19) is the primordial garden where the first created air of human beings is placed. The garden is therefore also among God's creations and the theatre in which the initial human drama unfolded. At a symbolic level the garden represents the ideal environment in which the first humans subsisted, close to God and in balance and harmony with nature. In the account, the human trespass, the act of disobeying God's command, results in dismissal from the garden and a sojourn on earth. The promise of a return to the garden—that is, the promised abode of the hereafter—is held out as the ultimate destination of the human journey; but until the return, the garden remains an aspiration and expectation, even a memory, that enables the human imagination and creativity to recreate a space with spiritual meaning on earth. Among the main features of the garden in paradise is water, an oft-repeated reference in the Qur'an, which also refers to the four rivers that flow in paradise (47:15)—rivers of water, milk, honey, and wine. Another is the ideal of reflection, tranquillity and repose—the universal greeting in paradise being *salaam*: peace!

This evocative, subtle, and richly symbolic historicised garden is the promised home of the righteous and overwhelmingly, the joy of knowing that they have pleased God, and that he is pleased with them. According to the Qur'an, the return to God is the supreme state of spiritual knowledge and joy.

One of the patterns that came to dominate the design of these gardens, though not exclusively, was the *chahar bagh*—the four fold garden, often linked to the Qur'anic allusion to the four rivers of paradise. The Mughal gardens are a fine example and extension of this style. The *chahar bagh* synthesises the key elements of nature that come together to shape the designed space: water, geometry, greenery and light as they interact with the different materials and designs that shape the landscape.

The Shalimar Gardens, a UNESCO World Heritage Site, is located in Lahore and was commissioned by Shah Jahan in 1637. The form of the garden is inspired by the model of the *chahar bagh*, set within an enclosure consisting of gardens, with a narrow rectangular terrace in between them. Each garden is divided by flower-beds and canals which provide water for the whole garden. White marble pavilions are dotted all over the gardens. The gardens are laid out along three descending terraces, each coming into view as one progresses from south to north. Each of these terraces is named to represent an act of giving, of joy, of well-being and of life itself. Over four hundred fountains send ripples of water, shimmering in the sunlight, creating through the gentleness of their sound as well as silence, an atmosphere of exuberance and delight that is echoed in much of the poetry and prose written in praise of the gardens. The total effect of the movement, harmony and designed flow is captured as the water cascades down across the terraces, following geometric rhythms and lending the four-squared vista a calm, yet palpable dignity of form and feeling.

In addition to the pavilions, other structures in the complex include chambers for the Emperor and his family, a *hammam*, or bath, a Great Hall, as well as decorated entrances and minarets. Historical records and modern practice suggest that a wide variety of trees, fruits and plants were grown in the gardens, including apples, peaches, oranges, almonds, apricots and mulberries, as well as poplars, cypresses and other shrubs, that have always been full of song birds.

Historical accounts indicate how pleased the Emperor Shah Jahan was with the garden and the serene atmosphere that he, his family and his courtiers could enjoy. The pavilions, in particular, provided privacy and shaded vantage points to view parts of the garden.

The Shalimar Garden, as other Mughal gardens, inspired poetry and literature, laden with symbolic references to the harmony of form and essence, the purity of water, the profusion of life, the transient and created nature of life, pointing ultimately to each individual's destiny and the remembrance of whence he originated. Thus, while the heritage of such gardens is inseparable from the ecological aspirations that we all share, they also mirror spiritual and human values that transcend time and space.

**PROFESSOR AZIM NANJI**
DIRECTOR OF THE INSITUTE OF ISMAILI STUDIES
LONDON, UNITED KINGDOM

# SHALIMAR BAGH

SRINAGAR, JAMMU & KASHMIR INDIA

SHALIMAR BAGH OR "THE ABODE OF LOVE" IS A 17TH CENTURY PERSIAN GARDEN BUILT BY THE EMPEROR JAHANGIR (REIGN 1605–1627) FOR HIS WIFE, NUR JAHAN IN 1616. IT WAS THEIR SUMMER RESIDENCE AND IS THE MOST CELEBRATED OF ROYAL GARDENS. THE GARDEN COMPRISES SEVERAL TERRACES LINKED BY WATER CHANNELS; THESE ARE SURROUNDED BY POOLS WHICH ARE ACCESSED VIA STEPPING STONES. THE HIGHEST OF THESE TERRACES WAS RESERVED EXCLUSIVELY FOR THE ROYAL LADIES OF THE COURT AND HOUSES A BLACK PAVILION IN THE CENTRE OF A RECTANGULAR POOL. THE NEXT LEVEL DOWN WAS KNOWN AS THE EMPEROR'S GARDEN AND THE LOWEST LEVEL WAS CONSIDERED THE PUBLIC GARDENS. WATER WOULD CASCADE FROM EVERY WALL DOWN TO THE NEXT LEVEL AND AT NIGHT OIL LAMPS WOULD BE PLACED IN THE CREVICES GIVING A SHIMMERING EFFECT AS WATER RAN OVER THEM. WHILE MANY OF THE ORIGINAL CANALS ARE NOW FILLED IN, THE PAVILION HAS BEEN RESTORED AND WATER STILL FLOWS DOWN THROUGH THE GARDEN AND ITS TERRACES.

Apart from being great builders who produced such masterpieces as the Taj Mahal and Red Fort in Agra, the Red Fort in Delhi, Humayun's Tomb and many other monuments, the Mughals also had a special love for gardens. Perhaps this was strengthened by the descriptions of the Islamic heaven in which gardens and fountains played a major part. Kashmir, of course, is a valley of unparallel beauty and was deeply loved by the Mughals. In particular the Emperor Jahangir used to visit Kashmir every year, and it was he who laid out the famous garden known as Shalimar Bagh in 1616 for his beloved wife the beautiful Empress Nur Jahan, covering an area of approximately 539 x 182 metres.

There is a traditional belief that much earlier King Pravarsena II, who founded Srinagar, had built a villa there around which the Shalimar village grew. Laid out in classical perfection, the Shalimar Garden is designed in several terraces with magnificent *chinar* trees on either side of the polished stones canal that flows through the centre of the Garden supplied with water from the Harwan reservoir. The fourth terrace was once reserved for royal ladies. It has a pavilion built of black stone in the centre of the tank, which was used as a banquet hall.

Shalimar Bagh has an air of solitude and quietude, and its rows of amazing fountains and shaded lined trees seem to retire towards the snow-dressed mountains. There are fountains all along at each level, so that when the Garden is in full bloom and the fountains are playing, it does take on an almost heavenly ambience. The origins of Mughal gardens can be traced back to the adoption of Persian culture including religion, art, architecture, script and language, and it would be correct to say that Mughal gardens in Kashmir can be viewed as a branch of Islamic garden history. Along with Shalimar there are two other famous Mughal gardens nearby, Nishat and Chashmashahi.

During the Dogra rule of my ancestors, Shalimar became a favourite picnic spot. I recall that as a child I used to visit there at least twice during the season when the garden was reserved for us and the general public was not allowed in. I still remember floating small paper boats on the rivulet and looking up at the sky through the mighty *chinar* trees with a sense of awe and wonder.

The Garden itself overlooks a magnificent view of the Dal Lake, and is known as one of the most romantic places in the world. Thomas Moore, in his poem *Lalla Rookh*, writes about "pale hands I love beside the Shalimar" which also became a song. Despite all the tension and turmoil that, unfortunately, has gripped the beautiful valley, the Shalimar Garden remains an oasis of peace and beauty and a tribute to the aesthetic sensibility of the Emperor Jahangir. Millions of tourists from all over India and the world visit it every year, and it is a favourite picnic spot for residents of Srinagar on Sundays and holidays. A sound and light show is held here every evening between May and October in the tourist season.

**H.H. MAHARAJAH OF KASHMIR, DR. KARAN SINGH**
MEMBER OF THE RAJYA SABHA (THE UPPER HOUSE OF PARLIAMENT)
NEW DELHI, INDIA

# NISHAT BAGH

SRINAGAR, JAMMU & KASHMIR INDIA

"THE GARDEN OF JOY OR BLISS", OR NISHAT BAGH, IS THE MOST DRAMATIC OF MUGHAL GARDENS IN KASHMIR AND THE LARGEST. SET ON THE BANKS OF LAKE DAL, WITH THE ZABARWAN MOUNTAINS AS ITS BACKDROP, THIS 17TH CENTURY PERSIAN GARDEN WAS DESIGNED BY NUR JAHAN'S BROTHER ASAF KHAN, THEN PRIME MINISTER, IN 1633. THE EMPEROR, SHAH JAHAN (REIGN 1628-1658) FELL IN LOVE WITH THESE GARDENS AND, FOR A BRIEF TIME, IN A FIT OF PIQUE, BECAUSE OWNERSHIP WAS NOT GIVEN TO HIM, TURNED THE WATER OFF TO THE GARDENS. ORIGINALLY DESIGNED WITH 12 TERRACES REPRESENTING THE SIGNS OF THE ZODIAC, LIFTING UP TOWARDS THE MOUNTAINS, THE LOWER TERRACES ARE NOW NO LONGER VISIBLE. THE WIDE CENTRAL CANAL AND WATER CHUTES ENSURE THAT THE WATER RUNS DOWN THE TERRACES IN WIDE CHANNELS AND CARVED STONE RAMPS. FOUNTAINS ARE STUDDED THROUGHOUT THE TERRACES AND FLOWER BEDS FULL OF MARIGOLDS, POPPIES, PANSIES, ROSES AND LILIES ARE AT EVERY LEVEL.

When I close my eyes and think of India, huge swathes of pink and orange flowers drift before me and I can almost smell the sweet, intoxicating scent of jasmine and frangipani. I can hear the trumpeting of elephants and the laughter of all my friends because, in my dreams, I am often back in Jodphur, amidst the frenzy and the joy of my own Indian wedding.

Most of my wedding celebrations took place outdoors and I fell in love with the charm of all the gardens in which we were lucky enough to celebrate. One party, my *Mendhi*, was in the gardens of the Umaid Bhawan Palace. I was staying in the Maharani suite, which has a beautiful, long and shady terrace, overlooking the stunning symmetrical patterns of the gardens. As I dressed in my jewel-encrusted sari, I could see gardeners laying out patterns of marigolds and lighting candles all the way down the sweeping steps. Different coloured bushes of bougainvillea are perfectly spaced and sculpted and my son, Damian, thought he was in a Hide and Seek paradise. Centre stage is a marble pavilion, in which I had my hands and feet painted in henna. The pavilion was hung with long garlands of lilies and a wonderful dancer from Lahore danced for us amongst the pillars.

There is a wonderful 11th century fort to the west of Jodphur, called Nagaur. We had a party amongst the ruins and were overwhelmed by the magnificence and scale of the gardens, all of which are in the process of being restored. There are huge, Mughal-style terraces which are exquisitely laid out, with fountains, pools and crossing patterns of waterways. We arranged tens of thousands of red chillies in geometric patterns to continue the theme. Nagaur Fort is possibly the most romantic place I have ever visited and our whole wedding party stayed overnight in tents. We filled each tent with strings of jasmine and it was hard to tear ourselves away the next day.

Wherever I go in India, I always notice the amazing attention to detail in gardens, regardless of whether they're of Persian or European influence, or uniquely Indian. I enjoy them all. In Bombay, my mother-in-law has a mixture of low, intricately patterned box hedging, sweet peas and palm trees, thus neatly covering all bases!

**ELIZABETH HURLEY**
ACTRESS, MODEL, DESIGNER
LONDON, UNITED KINGDOM

# THE ROCK GARDEN
## CHANDIGARH, PUNJAB/HARYANA INDIA

THE LIFE WORK OF ONE MAN, THE ROCK GARDEN IN CHANDIGARH IS AN INCREDIBLE FANTASYLAND COMPRISING IDIOSYNCRATIC SCULPTURE, WINDING PATHS, MOSAIC COURTYARDS AND DEEP GORGES. IT WAS STARTED 50 YEARS AGO BY NEK CHAND, WHO CLEARED A SMALL PIECE OF JUNGLE TO MAKE HIMSELF A GARDEN. COLLECTING WASTE AND RUBBISH OFF THE STREETS, HE RECYCLED THIS MATERIAL, CREATING ORIGINAL SCULPTURES, BOUNDARIES AND PATHWAYS. BY 1976 THE CITY AUTHORITIES, LARGELY FORCED BY PUBLIC OPINION, GAVE NEK CHAND A GRANT TO CONTINUE HIS OUTSTANDING WORK. A COMPLETE CONTRAST TO LE CORBUSIER'S REGULAR LAYOUT OF THE CITY ITSELF, THE ROCK GARDEN NOW INCLUDES SOME 14 COURTYARDS LINKED BY WALKWAYS, BUILDINGS, WATERFALLS AND STREAMS. THOUSANDS OF SCULPTURES COVERED IN MOSAICS CAN BE FOUND IN ALMOST EVERY CORNER OF THIS GARDEN, MAKING THIS WHOLE GARDEN AN EXTRAORDINARY ARTISTIC ACHIEVEMENT.

Within the city of Chandigarh, India, in a striking contrast to the modernist geometry of its design, lies the whimsical collection of rocks and urban waste transformed into sculpture, space and form, known as the Rock Garden.

The Rock Garden is not a garden in the conventional sense: it is not made up of vegetation, of trees and plants, but of inorganic material such as scrap and rock. Neither is it designed by a professional landscape architect nor by the course of nature: it is an amorphous collection of waste material modelled into space, as a hobby, by a passionate man. It was never intended to be a garden or, for that matter, have any formal spatial attributes, but emerged out of the random agglomeration of waste material. Irrespective of these contradictions, the rock garden has found its own identity in a city that is referred to as the 'mecca of architecture.'

While the designs of the master architect Le Corbusier were being translated into a new city, a road inspector in charge of a construction store was stealthily pursuing his hobby of transforming waste material and rocks into sculptures. As the urban form of the city was being announced by perhaps the most well-known experiment in architecture and planning, the naive and secret hobby of Nek Chand was incubating a contrasting space that would become one of the most visited places in the country.

Nek Chand worked clandestinely in the woods at night, by the light of 'burning tyres', risking imprisonment, to turn trash into treasure. A childhood dream of a city of gods and goddesses, *'nagri of devis* and *devatas'*, he created a surrealistic environment that has shades of Antonio Gaudi's Casa Mila in Barcelona and images of Alice in Wonderland rolled together. On discovery of his kingdom, though illegally built, it was recognised for its artistic endevour and preserved from being razed to the ground for not confirming to the strict master planning of Chandigarh.

The Rock Garden is a large collection of natural rock forms, sculptures, and architectural structures laid out within forty acres of labyrinthine chambers. The garden is, in reality, a large and complex labyrinth, with paths, gateways, steps, waterfalls, courtyards, porches and buildings. Set in the tributaries of a seasonal stream that flowed into a forest near the monumental design of the capitol complex of Corbusier, the topography of the land has been used to create a dramatic sequence of spaces or chambers. Each chamber is designed around a theme and open into each other through a series of low arches that dramatically unfold the architectural experience. Each chamber portrays a different aspect of Nek Chand's dream kingdom, featuring hundreds of animals, birds and human beings.

The garden proceeds in a chronological order of its creation, and in the unfolding, shows the process of Nek Chand's creation. Starting with a few natural forms and found objects like mis-shapen rocks, to minor landscape modification, finally leading to a large scale architectural environment. This phase of the garden constitutes vistas of landscaping, arranged through a series of courtyards patterned from refuse such as plastic machine parts, ceramic tiles, bits of plate, bangles, old shoes, hats, rags, broken pots & dishes, tiles, bottles, bicycles, dolls, birds nests, as well as human hair from barber shops.

The second phase of the garden consists of a playground for the entertainment of the 'elevated souls in heaven who found a place once again on earth.' Arranged in courts having waterfall, canal, an open air theatre, a miniature village, these architectural spaces have become over the years an interactive space, where plays, dance and music performances, even fashion shows, are held. In another section, Nek Chand created a miniature village with shops, houses, paths, temples and a cascading waterfall. This make-believe world is enhanced further by the trees, vegetation and birds that inhabit the remaining forest. Hundreds of birds live in the garden, using the small nooks and crannies as nesting places.

Phase III, Nek Chand's work has become monumental in scale: life-sized horses and camels, aquarium and an open-air theatre. Children and visitors to the garden can climb up and down these figures and actually experience and participate with Nek Chand's creative genius. The heart of this section of the garden is the "great swings," dozens of swings that hang from huge concrete arches resembling ancient Roman aqueducts.

The recycling of waste has been an important part of the Rock Garden since its inception. In addition to creating a magical respite for the local population and visitors, the Rock Garden has the added benefit of ridding Chandigarh of heaps of its urban and industrial trash. Nek Chand set up collection centres throughout the city. His biggest suppliers were venues generating lots of waste; hospitals, hotels, and restaurants. He also set up local networks through which broken ceramics, rags, tiles and other refuse were funneled to the garden and there recycled.

By reinvesting waste and imbuing it with an aesthetic appeal, balance and harmony, a sculptural park has been created. Nek Chand has demonstrated the harmony between man-made waste and nature: "It is my belief that any conflict between nature's will and man's design is bound to lead to an overall destruction. The dimensions of the essential harmony between man and nature can be economic, social, political and aesthetic. My own effort is to explore the aesthetic dimension. The natural environment, trees, water, soil, birds, rocks are the major participants in my work."

Though designed unconsciously, the Rock Garden possesses high sensibilities of architecture and landscape design. A key aesthetic feature of the garden is the sense of compression and expansion of space. In moving from one section of the garden to another through narrow passageways into broad open courtyards, the visitor experiences a varying sequence of spaces. The deliberate manipulation of the scale of the spaces and forms create a sense of movement and enclosure. The play with scale, light, and materials creates anticipation and surprise. The rhythmic unfolding of spaces gently leads the visitor through the garden, revealing specific works and sculptures at particular times.

The journey through these spaces is filled with dramatic scenes expressed through playful sculptures made out of 'everyday' materials and thematically arranged to construct narratives of delight and mystery.

Much like a folk tale, the Rock Garden uses ordinary urban waste to create an extraordinary spatial experience; equally as a process of re-use as well as a product of spatial design.

**VIKRAM LALL**
PARTNER & PRINCIPAL ARCHITECT OF LALL & ASSOCIATES
NEW DELHI, INDIA

# HUMAYUN'S TOMB GARDEN
## NEW DELHI, DELHI INDIA

MAGNIFICENTLY RESTORED BY THE AGA KHAN TRUST FOR CULTURE IN 2003, HUMAYUN'S TOMB AND GARDENS IS A 16TH CENTURY MUGHAL GARDEN AND IS THE FINEST SURVIVING EXAMPLE OF THIS TYPE OF ARCHITECTURE IN INDIA. THE TOMB WAS COMMISSIONED BY HAMIDA BANU BEGUM, THE WIDOW OF THE 2ND MUGHAL EMPEROR, HUMAYUN (REIGN 1530-1540, 1555-1556) IN 1562 AND TOOK 8 YEARS TO COMPLETE. IT INCORPORATES THE TOMB OF EMPEROR HUMAYUN, BUILT IN A SIMILAR STYLE TO THE TAJ MAHAL IN AGRA, SURROUNDED BY A GEOMETRICALLY PERFECT PERSIAN STYLE *CHAHAR BAGH* GARDEN. IT IS THE FIRST EXAMPLE OF A TOMB GARDEN TO BE FOUND IN INDIA AND IS NOW A LISTED UNESCO WORLD HERITAGE SITE. THE GARDEN ITSELF IS 36 SQUARES DIVIDED BY A GRID OF WATER AND IT IS THANKS TO THE REMARKABLE RESTORATION WORK THAT WATER ONCE AGAIN FLOWS THROUGH THE WATERCOURSES IN THE GARDENS AND THAT HIBISCUS, LEMONS AND POMEGRANATE ARE FLOWERING.

Through the early morning mist, a pure white marble dome is silhouetted against the rising sun. Plumes of feathery coconut palms stand guard at its flanks. A wave of gently spreading crowns of Tamarind, Neem, and Mango trees surround it, like an island in the ocean. A high rampart wall veils the secret garden from the outside world. For this is the last resting place of the Mughal Emperor Humayun.

His tomb lies in Delhi, the ancient seat of the Mughal Empire, a dynastic rule founded by Humayun's father Babur in 1526. Humayun's reign was troubled by warfare and he went into exile in Persia, where he immersed himself in art and literature. With the help of Shah Tahmasp I, then ruler of Persia, he regained Delhi in 1555 ending the Sur rule.

On his triumphant return, he brought from Persia artists to paint exquisite miniatures; noble poets to stock his library; and the finest architects of Bukhara and Herat to rebuild his capital. Humayun is often dismissed for his fondness for the arts and for enjoying smoking his hookah but he deserves greater credit for bringing Timurid culture to India.

Only six months after retaking Delhi, the Emperor tragically fell to his death from his library steps. His devoted wife Haji Begam turned to the Herat architect Sayyed Mohammad, who drew up plans for a tomb conceived as a Persian *chahar bagh* garden, a square walled garden with a four-fold plan intersected by water courses and paths lined with trees. This plan is deeply symbolic as it physically illustrates paradise as described in the Qur'an with its flowing subterranean rivers, cool relaxing pavilions and abundance of fruit- and nut-bearing trees, where water purifies the soul. Indeed it is rather an appropriate metaphor for a garden of remembrance and ideal for Haji Begam to express eternal love for her late husband.

Humayun's tomb was the first great Mughal monument to be built in India and one which sets a precedent for the great tombs of the Mughal Emperors which followed, reaching their zenith in the perfection of his great grandson Shah Jahan's Taj Mahal.

At the heart of the mausoleum lies Humayun's white marble cenotaph in an octagonal sepulchre, dappled with light from an intricately patterned stone *jali* (window screen). It is set within a classic nine-fold geometrical plan, surmounted by a vast bulbous onion-shaped dome and sits on a broad raised terrace housing the crypt of royal tombs. Each of the four symmetrical facades is centred by a great pointed arch which, combined with the lower projecting octagonal corner pavilions, imbues the tomb with a baroque sense of movement. The drama is heightened by *chattris* (cupolas) on the parapets, which carry the eye up to the dome, linking the temporal world with the spiritual. The visual feast is enriched by fine building materials: red sandstone quarried near Agra is outlined by white marble from Rajasthan, drawing ornate geometric patterns across the surface and highlighted by other chromatic details such as stars and marble panels.

Entering the walled garden through the West Gate, I am struck by the sheer majesty of the mausoleum in front of me in the centre of the formally laid out gardens. Sandy paths radiate from each side of the tomb to the four cardinal points, terminating in pavilions. Each path is bisected by a narrow channel of water that flows into square or octagonal pools. Under the cool shade of a grove of Pilkhan trees in the south parterre a courting couple sit reflecting by the pool, nearby birds fill the air with their songs and a pair of peacocks strut elegantly across the well-watered grass. In the North parterre kites leave their roosts in the Pipal trees to circle the sky on the rising thermals, looking down on this tranquil oasis.

Amid such peace and picturesque splendour it is difficult to imagine some of the turbulent and critical historical events that happened here. Humayun's great great grandson, Prince Dara Shikoh was brutally murdered in the vicinity of the tomb on the orders of his younger brother, Aurangzeb, who was after the throne, and his severed head sent to his imprisoned father Shah Jahan.

Two centuries later, after the British quashed the Indian Mutiny in 1857, the defeated Emperor Bahadur Shah took refuge in the crypt with his ten sons. He was discovered there by Lieutenant Hodson. His sons were shot and the deposed Emperor and his wife were exiled to Rangoon.

After the Mutiny many Mughal buildings were destroyed as they were felt to undermine the British Raj. Others, such as Humayun's Tomb, remained neglected. My great uncle Lord Curzon, Viceroy of India (1899-1905) had an enormous respect for India's ancient monuments and devoted much of his time and energy to conserving them. He is chiefly remembered for saving the Taj Mahal and restoring its garden. He also found time to restore Humayun's tomb, although he exclaimed to his Amercian wife Mary Leiter in 1905, "You remember Humayun's tomb? I had the garden restored, the water channels dug out and refilled and the whole place restored to its pristine beauty. I went to England last summer and, the eye of the master being away, the whole place has been allowed to revert. The garden has been let to a native and is now planted with turnips and the work of four years is thrown away!" Lord Curzon's efforts however, were not in vain and the Archaeological Survey of India (ASI), which he instigated, is the largest caretaker of historic sites in the world.

In 2003 the ASI undertook an extensive programme of restoration generously sponsored by the Aga Khan Trust for Culture. The grant enabled a thorough archaeological excavation and historical research and the reinstatement of the hydraulic system and water channels. Wells were cleared, plats levelled and paths re-laid. Undergrowth and inappropriate planting such as the Ashoka trees were removed. Replanting was based on Mughal texts with an emphasis on citrus species. This was augmented with flowering and sweet-smelling shrubs, including Jasminium, Hibiscus, Harsingar, Chandnee, and Anar.

Beauty and order has been restored and it is a joy to see water flowing through the garden again. What might Lord Curzon have made of it? I feel sure that it would have earned his highest praise for giving the first imperial mausoleum of the Mughal dynasty back its beautiful setting and its dignity. An earthly paradise has been regained.

**HON. JAMES CURZON**
LANDOWNER AND HISTORIAN
LONDON, UNITED KINGDOM

# SAHELION-KI-BARI

UDAIPUR, RAJASTHAN  INDIA

ALSO KNOWN AS "THE GARDEN OF THE MAIDS OF HONOUR", SAHELION-KI-BARI IS AN 18TH CENTURY HINDU RAIN GARDEN AND WAS BUILT BY MAHARANA SANGRAM SINGH II (REIGN 1710-1734). IT IS SAID THAT IT WAS ORIGINALLY DESIGNED AS A COOL RETREAT FOR THE 48 MAIDS WHO ACCOMPANIED THE MAHARANA'S WIFE AS PART OF HIS DOWRY. LATER A PAVILION OF RAIN FOUNTAINS WAS COMMISSIONED BY MAHARANA BHOPAL SINGHJI TO CREATE THE ILLUSION OF DANCING MAIDS. FLOOD DAMAGE IN THE 19TH CENTURY LED TO MASSIVE RECONSTRUCTION BY MAHARANA FATEH SINGH. THE FOUNTAINS WITHIN THE GARDEN ARE REMINISCENT OF TRADITIONAL ENGLISH, SOME MADE OF COLOURED CAST IRON WHILE OTHERS, LIKE THE WHITE MARBLE *CHATTRI* FOUNTAIN IN THE CENTRE, DATE VERY MUCH FROM HINDU DESIGN OF THE TIME AND REFLECT AN ERA WHEN INDIAN GARDENS INCORPORATED A LOT OF WHIMSICAL ENGLISH ELEMENTS INTO THEM. PALM-LINED MARBLE PATHS LEAD TO EXTENSIVE LAWNS, SHADY WALKS, AND FRUITS TREES. THE ROSE GARDEN FEATURES OVER 100 VARIETIES AND AN ENDLESS ASSORTMENT OF FOUNTAINS AND POOLS MAINTAIN THE CHARM OF THESE GARDENS.

India has always been known as a country of diversity and it is through this diversity that we have grown. We are the birth-place of four religions; our geography ranges from the soaring Himalayan ranges to the Deccan Plateau, the floodplains of the Indus and the Thar Desert; historically we have seen a myriad of civilisations develop and prosper on our soil and it is the vestiges of what they have left behind that have made us grow and prosper even further as a nation.

From the grandeur of the Taj Mahal to the royal gardens of Shalimar Bagh, we are a nation that has always celebrated love. Sahelion-ki-Bari in Udaipur is another fine example of this outpouring of love and of our celebration of the beauty that surrounds us all, the beauty and harmony of nature.

This 18th Century pleasure park, also known as the Gardens of the Maids, combines the tranquility of nature with the harmony achieved through technology: from the flower beds, towering trees and clipped lawns to the marble and cast-iron fountains, we see the blend between the old and the new. The symmetry found here, nearly 300 years old, is still relevant and cherished today. There is a distinct balance here between both the spiritual and the functional.

It is through the preservation of this wonderfully complex history of ours and our under-standing of it that, as a nation, we will continue to develop, both spiritually and economically. Our future prosperity, in all realms of our lives, is marked forever by our past and our appreciation of it. It is these cultural artifacts that have been left to us, like Sahelion-ki-Bari, that root us as a nation, as Indians. It is also these incredible landmarks that bring the diversity of people from all walks of life together in a common appreciation of beauty and tradition.

**H.H. PRINCESS MADHAVI SCINDIA**
RAJMATA OF GWALIOR
NEW DELHI, INDIA

# THEOSOPHICAL GARDEN

ADYAR, MADRAS/CHENNAI INDIA

LOCATED IN THE ADYAR NEIGHBOURHOOD OF CHENNAI, THE SPRAWLING GARDENS OF THE THEOSOPHICAL SOCIETY ARE ADJACENT TO THE ADYAR RIVER. FOUNDED IN NEW YORK IN 1875, THE SOCIETY HEADQUARTERS WAS MOVED TO INDIA IN 1882 WHEN THE FOUNDERS ACQUIRED THIS LAND, FORMERLY KNOWN AS HUDDLESTONE GARDENS. ORIGINALLY COVERING JUST 27 ACRES, BY 1911 THE GROUNDS HAD EXPANDED, THROUGH PURCHASE OF ADJOINING LOTS, TO 253 ACRES INCLUDING THE BLAVATSKY GARDENS, OLCOTT GARDENS, BESANT GARDENS, DAMODAR GARDENS, BESANT GROVE AND THE ALSACE GROVE. ONE OF THE GREAT ATTRACTIONS HERE IS THE 400-YEARS OLD BANYAN TREE WHOSE SPREADING BRANCHES COVER AN IMMENSE AREA OF 4,180SQ M (44,993 SQ FT). THIS TREE IS BELIEVED TO BE THE SECOND OLDEST BANYAN TREE IN INDIA.

The Theosophical Gardens in Chennai evokes many memories. I remember my first visit to it, which was also my first visit to Madras in South India, as a child of ten. This was on a family summer vacation to Ceylon. Our return to distant Lucknow in the north, was planned via Madras, and under the instruction of our father, my mother took their three offspring to see the famous 400-year old Banyan tree in the Theosophical Gardens in Adyar.

It was enchantment at first sight. Quite indelibly imprinted in my mind's eye is the forest that was this Banyan tree, reputedly the second largest in India, after the one in Kolkata. The many tertiary roots stood solid and formed a veritable jungle. I remember families picnicking in groups under the Banyan tree's vast green canopy. To us children, it was impossible to believe that the many supposed trunks were part of the same tree. (Sadly, the main trunk was severely uprooted by a cyclone in 1989. Various attempts to save it were futile. Today, the tree stands on the strength of its many secondary roots, now stout trunks).

This was an incredible experience and our second such encounter during that summer of '59. In Ceylon, we had visited the famous Banyan tree in Peradeniya, the Botanical Gardens in Kandy. That Banyan tree had been even larger than the one in the Theosophical Gardens. For years, we referred to this summer vacation in Ceylon and Madras as "The Banyan Tree Holiday." It was to be many years later that Ceylon would become Sri Lanka and Madras would be called Chennai and the 'Banyan Tree' would be a famous chain of holiday spas.

It was also many years later that I began a serious interest in the Theosophical Gardens. This was because of a great interest in the Theosophical Society, which is set in these large and tranquil gardens. In the early 1980's, whilst researching the work and life of Sir Edwin Lutyens, the architect and planner of New Delhi, the Imperial Capital of British India, I came upon several accounts of his wife, Emily's interest in the Theosophical Society. She became a Theosophist in 1912, the same year that Sir Edwin Lutyens was appointed the architect of New Delhi. This was most unusual. Emily, nee Lytton, the daughter of Lord Lytton, who had been Viceroy of India from 1876 to 1880, was greatly influenced by Annie Besant, the then president of the Theosophical Society and an exceptional woman in every respect.

I read many accounts. The Theosophical Society was formed to facilitate and encourage the study of comparative religions and philosophy. The society was founded by Madame Blavatsky and Col. Olcott in the USA in 1875 and later moved to Adyar in 1882. Apart from shrines of all faiths and the peaceful Garden of Remembrance, there is a 95-year old library which has a very good collection of rare Oriental manuscripts, written on palm leaves and parchment. The garden and the society are integral to each other. The Society was also a great advocate of the cremation of dead bodies. These Hindu customs of sepulture were considered "barbaric" in the west, in the late 19th century.

I, of course, was fascinated and promptly went down south to investigate thoroughly the headquarters of the Theosophical Society, housed in these unique gardens.

Since that second visit in the 80's, I have visited the Theosophical Gardens on several occasions, particularly whilst working on the documentation of the Governor's Residence, also situated in Adyar, and built around the same period as the principal buildings of the Society in the Theosophical Gardens.

Each visit reveals more and more treasures—about the major metaphysical discourses and meditation courses that have been held under the huge 60,000 sq. foot canopy of the 'Adyar' Banyan tree. (Incidentally, the name 'banyan' was given to the tree by the early English visitors to India. They saw Banias (traders) of the locality assemble in the shade of this tree to conduct a sort of stock exchange.) Shrines, representing all the major religions in the world, are housed here. The tranquil Theosophical Gardens is a true paradise, a balm to the senses. These Gardens are exceptional and unique.

**SUNITA KOHLI**
INTERIOR DESIGNER, ARCHITECTURAL RESTORER AND FURNITURE MANUFACTURER
NEW DELHI, INDIA

# ROYAL BOTANIC GARDENS, PERADENIYA

## KANDY, CENTRAL  SRI LANKA

ESTABLISHED BY THE BRITISH IN 1921, THE SITE OF THE ROYAL BOTANIC GARDENS, PERADENIYA HAS IMMENSE HISTORICAL VALUE AS FROM 1371 VARIOUS KINGS OF KANDY, SRI LANKA RESIDED AND RULED FROM PALACES AT PERADENIYA. COVERING NEARLY 60 HECTARES, THE GARDEN WAS FIRST CULTIVATED BY ALEXANDER MOON WHO, LATER, WAS TO PUBLISH HIS *CATALOGUE OF CEYLON PLANTS* COVERING MORE THAN 1,000 SPECIES. TODAY THE GARDEN BOASTS MORE THAN 4,000 SPECIES OF PLANT INCLUDING A WIDE VARIETY OF PALMS, ORCHIDS, FERNS AND GYMNOSPERMS. A STUNNING AVENUE OF ROYAL PALMS LEADS THE VISITOR TO THE MANY SITES OF THE GARDEN INCLUDING THE GIANT BANYAN TREE WHOSE BRANCHES LOOM AND STRETCH OVERHEAD AND A SPICE GARDEN HOSTING A PLETHORA OF MATURE SAMPLES.

Gardens, like music, have distinct tones and personalities, defined by colours, shapes and arrangements. As visitors, we participate with our own melodies of thoughts, murmurings and chatter. These visual dialogues of landscape embraced by notes of nature, when played in harmony, create unique symphonies that can transport us beyond our worlds. Peradeniya does just that.

The Peradeniya Gardens, covering over 147 acres, is a collection of landscapes, predominantly with differing hues of green, silver and beige, which are sculpted by ancient trees and interrupted seasonally with bright blooms. It is a garden of classical chords, traditional and soothing in its aesthetic, with a seemingly endless embrace of green. The gardens represent continuum of time, environmental peace and preservation, patience and perseverance, a sanctuary from the staccato world which we otherwise occupy.

In keeping with the variety offered by royal gardens, Peradeniya presents contrasting responses through its landscapes: intimacy against openness, simplicity against grandeur, all accommodated into a sprawling landscape of subtle changes in colour, punctuated by strong tropical sensibilities.

Legend has it that the Indian Prince Wijeya married a local tribal queen, Kuweni. After bearing him children, she was expelled from the palace and found refuge in a fruit orchard, the predecessor to these gardens. She was a weaver and thus, the word "Pera", which is a derivative from the Sinhala word *Pehera* meaning "cotton weaving", was assigned to the gardens. *Deniya* is a Sinhala word for "meadow".

Thereafter, from the 14th century, the gardens were used by kings, beginning with King Vikrama Bahu III, who kept court there. Some later kings constructed temporary residences. One can imagine why these monarchs wished to be cocooned by the tranquility and vastness of these 'pleasure gardens' which provided an idyllic escape from external turmoil. (More recently, the last Viceroy of India, Lord Mountbatten's Second World War headquarters was situated here.)

In the early 1800s, the area became the Royal Botanic Gardens accommodating a number of indigenous and new varieties of plants; with this the present park plan was born. Peradeniya is Sri Lanka's largest botanic garden, containing over 4,000 species of flora. The vast acreage is embraced on three sides by the Mahaweli River. Giant bamboos line those shores in select spots, with trunks resembling organ pipes that sprout to heights of up to 40 metres.

The atmosphere is serene even in the most inhabited of times. The tree-lined spaces absorb man-made cacophony. Carpets of lawn welcome and embrace, with distinct inner gardens. The Spice Garden has a representative selection of spices exported from Sri Lanka, including pepper, cardamon and nutmeg. Some of the oldest nutmeg trees, planted in 1840, still bear fruit and the garden spreads sensory delight with spice fragrances.

Numerous paths lead to varieties of floral pleasure and there is no road less travelled. The Great Lawn offers the Java Willow, (also known as the Java Fig Tree), with an umbrella of foliage covering 1,600 square metres, majestic from afar and protective when we stand underneath its myriad of branches and shade. Palm avenues are lined with perpendicular splendour: cabbage palms, double coconut palms, cannonball trees, and the exotic coco de mer which produces gargantuan coconuts, each fruit anywhere from 10 kg to 20 kg—not edible but resembling a Victor Hugo character.

The list of exotica goes on, woven into the vast and undulating landscape which ends only at the horizon. The symphony of this garden is fortunately available to all, offering sanctuary, inspiration and invigoration of spirit—as they have done for centuries.

**DATIN SHALINI AMERASINGHE GANENDRA**
FINE ARTS CONSULTANT & GALLERIST
KUALA LUMPUR, MALAYSIA

# THE BRIEF GARDEN

## KALAWILA, WESTERN  SRI LANKA

DESIGNED AND BUILT BY LANDSCAPE ARCHITECT AND ARTIST BEVIS BAWA, THE STUNNING BRIEF GARDEN AND THE HOUSE ARE AN OPEN MUSEUM. BORROWING STYLES FROM THE FORMAL EUROPEAN GARDEN, THE CHARM OF THE ORIENTAL GARDEN AND THE TROPICAL OPULENCE IN FLORA IN THIS REGION, BAWA ENSURED THAT THIS GARDEN REMAINS A MINI-PARADISE ON EARTH. THE LAND, APPARENTLY, WAS PURCHASED BY HIS FATHER FROM THE PROCEEDS OF A LEGAL BRIEF, HENCE THE NAME ADOPTED BY BEVIS. IT WAS PREVIOUSLY A RUBBER PLANTATION. IN 1920, BEVIS CLEARED THIS LAND AND CREATED A WORLD OF DIVERSE GARDEN STYLES AND PLANTINGS. PAVING IMPRINTED WITH LEAF PATTERNS, AN ITALIAN STYLE WATER STAIRCASE, JAPANESE GARDEN, AND EVEN AN EDIBLE GARDEN ARE JUST A SMALL PART OF THIS OASIS. BEVIS WAS ALSO VERY CLOSE TO DONALD FRIEND AND TODAY YOU WILL STILL SEE MUCH ARTWORK GIVEN BY FRIEND TO THE HOUSE AND GARDEN.

The gardens I remember are the gardens of my childhood. My family left Ceylon (as it was then) in 1961—part of the post-independence Tamil diaspora. I was just six years old at the time. Not for me the orchid house at the Royal Botanical Gardens in Peradeniya; not for me the manicured lawns and frangipani trees of Cinnamon Gardens in Colombo. This book celebrates the garden as a creation—something to look at and admire—but for me the garden was somewhere to play in. They may not have been "noble" but for this six-year-old they were playgrounds fit for a king!

My maternal grandmother's home in Welawatte, a suburb of Colombo, was typical of the houses built in the British colonial period—a small verandah, rusty-red half-tube tiles on the roof and shuttered windows to keep the heat of the day out of the rooms. The plot was not as generous as you might find in the wealthier parts of the city so every available piece of land seemed to be put to good use. There was a mango tree, a guava tree and the ubiquitous banana tree. But my favourite was the jambu tree.

Sometimes called the rose apple, in season its bell-shaped fruits hung like baubles on a Christmas tree just waiting to be plucked. One of my earliest memories is of my cousins—Mohan and Suresh—throwing handfuls of the fruits down to the rest of us. We were never patient enough to wait for the fruits to ripen so they tended to be rather sour. But, for our purposes, that was all the better. One of us would sneak into the kitchen—hopefully avoiding *amma-amma*, our grandmother—and return with a saucer of vinegar, salt and chilli powder. We had an instant pickle!

Growing fruit trees seems to have been something of an obsession that ran through both sides of my family. On the other side of the island, in the east, my father's mother was quietly famous for being one of the first to grow a grape vine in her garden. Imagine that! A grape vine being grown on Puliyan-tivu, ("Tamarind Island" because it was said to be shaped like a tamarind seed). Despite her loving care and attention, which included planting it in a pit filled with succulent cactus, the vine never delivered anything but small, sour grapes. Perhaps they, too, should have thought of pickling them!

Our family holidays were spent at my grandfather's retirement home in the village of Kalmunai, further down the coast from Puliyan-tivu. From his verandah we could see the Indian Ocean. His home on Rest House Road was easily found. There were three coconut trees in the front garden. They were a gift from my father to his father—*appa-appa*—to mark the year I was born, 1955. You might think that taking coconut trees to a seaside village is about as imaginative as offering booze to an alcoholic but these were the *kundira pol* variety—short enough, my father says, for a tall man to simply pluck the coconuts by hand.

I looked for the trees when I returned to Kalmunai as a BBC reporter just a few days after the Boxing Day tsunami in 2004. But I searched in vain. The little trees had been no match for the great tidal wave that had reduced so much of the village to rubble. The adult in me knew that the loss of the *kundira pol* trees was but a trifle in the devastation and misery that was all too obvious; the child in me grieved for the playground that was no more. As that wave receded into the Indian Ocean it had taken a part of my childhood with it.

**GEORGE ALAGIAH, OBE**
PRESENTER, BBC SIX O'CLOCK NEWS, WORLD NEWS TODAY
LONDON, UNITED KINGDOM

SOUTH EAST ASIA

As well as creating a living repository of local flora, the Queen Sirikit Botanic Garden conducts plant propagation programmes for selected species, and has programmes aimed at re-introducing endangered plant species back into the wild. An on-going project is the propagation of *Vanda coerulea,* known locally as Fa Mui, an endangered orchid specie with large light blue flowers native to northern Thailand, and its re-introduction back into its natural habitat. The propagation and commercialisation of this orchid specie by the botanic garden was so successful that poachers no longer bother seeking it out and collecting it from the forest.

The orchid nursery keeps a collection of rare orchids such as the colourful "Nimmanoradee" *(Eria amica),* named by Her Majesty the Queen after she was shown the plant in full bloom in the Northeastern Province of Loei in March of 1991. But the nursery also keeps in its collection a famous commercial white orchid that received the Award of Excellence by the Royal Horticultural Society as far back as 1958 known as "Queen Sirikit Cattleya." Developed by Black & Flory the extremely attractive white cattleya was named after Her Majesty.

The garden currently propagates a number of rare tree species. *Wrightia sirikitiae* in the Apocynaceae family, an extremely rare tree found only in hilly areas of Phrabuddhabat District in the Central Province of Lopburi, was discovered in 1972 and named after Her Majesty in 2001. Another rare new species the botanic garden is propagating is "Jampi Sirindhorn" *(Magnolia sirindhorniae)* in the Magnoliaceae family. Found in 1999 near Sapjampa village in Tha Luang District of the Province of Lopburi as well, "Jampi Sirindhorn" was named after Princess Sirindhorn, who herself is patron of a programme aimed at local plant species conservation. The flowering season for "Jampi Sirindhorn" is between September and December and its white flowers emit a sweet fragrance starting at dusk.

The development of the relatively young Queen Sirikit Botanic Garden is a work in progress and it is continually visited by horticultural experts in the Asia-Pacific region as well as local and foreign tourists. The Garden will also consider accepting serious volunteers willing to devote their time and energy to work on special projects. As Thailand's first botanic garden, Queen Sirikit Botanic Garden has gone a long way to establish a base from which to preserve local flora for future generations, but much more is to be done in the decades ahead to realise the full potential of the garden.

**DR. WORAPHAT ARTHAYUKTI**
SENIOR ASSOCIATE, KENAN INSTITUTE ASIA
BANGKOK, THAILAND

# NONG NOOCH TROPICAL BOTANICAL GARDEN

PATTAYA, CHONBURI THAILAND

OPENED IN 1980 THIS MAGICAL WONDERLAND COVERS 600 ACRES OF ROLLING HILLS AND VALLEYS. IT WAS CONCEIVED OF BY MRS. NONGNOOCH TANSACHA AFTER A TRIP ABROAD AND IS TRULY AN ECLECTIC MIX OF CULTURES AND STYLES BORROWED FROM ALMOST EVERY CENTURY AND ALMOST EVERY PART OF THE WORLD. FORMAL EUROPEAN GARDENS RESPLENDENT WITH CLASSICAL STATUES GIVE WAY TO FANTASTIC THAI TOPIARY, STRICT CASCADES REMINISCENT IN STYLE OF THE ITALIAN RENAISSANCE TO TALL COLONNADED HEDGES, ABSTRACT TOPIARY AND SWIRLING PSYCHEDELIC LAND ART TO CACTI, FERNS AND BONSAI—THERE IS EVEN AN ADAPTATION OF STONEHENGE HERE AND A REPLICA OF THE GARDENS OF VERSAILLES—AN ABSOLUTE FEAST FOR THE EYES. THE GROUNDS ARE NOW EQUIPPED WITH THAI-STYLE HOUSES, VILLAS, BANQUET AND SEMINAR HALLS, RESTAURANTS, A SWIMMING POOL, AND THAI CULTURAL PERFORMANCES ARE PRESENTED DAILY.

In this ever changing and complex world, it is such a great pleasure to be able to revel in the beauty of nature.

It is the natural environment that is enjoyed by people from all over the world, regardless of nationality, economic circumstances or beliefs. Nature is a rejuvenating arena for every generation. The realm of nature reminds us all that diversity can be celebrated, even embraced, and that there are some universally held values.

When I see a tropical paradise like Suan Nong Nooch, I am reminded again of how great visions can become reality, and a reality that is today enjoyed by thousands of visitors daily.

The grounds of Suan Nong Nooch encompass a multitude of gardens, each growing and thriving. From the lush plantings of palms and other tropical foliage in the Meadow gardens to the clipped and trimmed designs of the Thai Topiary Garden and the French Garden, the variety and abundance astound all who see it. Within the beautiful horticultural environment the visitor can also experience the cultural diversity of Thailand.

But Suan Nong Nooch is much more than a beautiful tourist attraction. It is committed to education, research, preservation and conservation of the environment. These are principles that should be upheld by all nations.

It is through the realms of a garden such as Suan Nong Nooch and the other gardens in this book that we can share our common vision of a better and more beautiful world, and become inspired to work towards this high goal.

**H.E. MR. NITYA PIBULSONGGRAM**
MINISTER OF FOREIGN AFFAIRS OF THE ROYAL KINGDOM OF THAILAND
BANGKOK, THAILAND

# THE LAKE GARDEN (TAMAN TASIK PERDANA)

JALAN PERDANA, KUALA LUMPUR  MALAYSIA

ESTABLISHED IN THE 1880'S THIS TROPICAL PARK IN THE HEART OF KUALA LUMPUR WAS THE BRAINCHILD OF ALFRED VENNING, THE BRITISH STATE TREASURER AT THE TIME. COVERING 92 HECTARES, THE PARK COMPRISES CLOSE-CROPPED LAWNS, AND CULTIVATED GARDENS. SET AROUND TWO LAKES, THE TROPICAL OASIS ALSO BOASTS A BUTTERFLY PARK, A BIRD PARK AND DEER GARDEN AS WELL AS NUMEROUS FLOWER BEDS, A HIBISCUS GARDEN AND AN ORCHID GARDEN. IT IS ALSO THE HOME OF THE MALAYSIAN NATIONAL MONUMENT, ONE OF THE WORLD'S LARGEST FREE-STANDING BRONZE SCULPTURES. HUGELY POPULAR AMONGST JOGGERS AND THOSE GOING FOR A MORE LEISURELY STROLL, THE LAKE GARDEN IS ALSO A REGULAR VENUE FOR MUSICAL AND CULTURAL PERFORMANCES AND IS A GREEN LUNG FOR AN EVER EXPANDING CITY.

Nature and man are inextricably linked. Where most think of this in terms of what we take from the land to survive, our links to nature are so much greater than just that.

Our environment moulds and guides us in so many ways: in design we constantly look towards the natural world for inspiration. Spiritually we seek a balance, a yin and yang to ensure harmony. When we meditate or are seeking other holistic treatment we look to nature to guide us.

The urban landscape of Kuala Lumpur has grown to such an extent that to find a natural retreat is not so easy. However, Taman Tasik Perdana, or The Lake Garden, in the heart of the city provides a perfect haven. From the first light of day you will find people performing their exercise there, from the calm of Tai Chi to much more vigorous aerobic activities.

However, it is not only a realm for exercise, it is also an arena for calm, for reading, writing, painting and even meditating.

Our busy, fast paced lives give us little time now to wonder at the glories of the natural world. This green oasis, like that of Hyde Park in London, gives all of us the opportunity to escape from the hustle and bustle of the day.

What is incredible in Malaysia is the way that all plants grow and thrive. Our rich natural jungles are absolute proof of that. In Taman Tasik Perdana we are shown this beyond doubt. The lush tropical foliage competes against the horizon of skyscrapers, contrasting the city streets with the fertile ground on which we live.

**DATO' PROFESSOR JIMMY CHOO, OBE**
FASHION DESIGNER
KUALA LUMPUR, MALAYSIA

# PUTRAJAYA BOTANICAL GARDEN (TAMAN BOTANI PUTRAJAYA)
PRECINT 1, PUTRAJAYA MALAYSIA

ESTABLISHED AS PART OF THE 230 ACRES OF WHAT WAS FORMERLY AGRICULTURAL LAND, THE BOTANICAL GARDEN WAS OPENED TO THE PUBLIC IN 2001 AND HAS BEEN DESIGNED AS A NATIONAL SANCTUARY FOR THE MALAYSIAN LIVING COLLECTION OF PLANT TAXONOMY. WITH MORE THAN 750 SPECIES OF PLANTS NATIVE TO 90 DIFFERENT COUNTRIES, INCLUDING THOSE FROM THE AFRICAN, TROPICAL AMERICAN AND ASIA-PACIFIC CONTINENTS, THE BOTANICAL GARDEN IS A MICROCOSM OF THE BREADTH AND DIVERSITY OF TROPICAL FLOWERING SPECIES. WITHIN THE GROUNDS YOU CAN FIND AN ISLAMIC GARDEN PAVILION WITH MOROCCAN INSPIRED ARCHITECTURE AND MASONRY WORK. THE GARDENS ARE ALSO A CENTRE FOR EDUCATION, RESEARCH AND CONSERVATION WITH NURSERIES, A HERBARIUM AND A SANCTUARY FOR LOCAL, RARE AND ENDANGERED SPECIES.

Growing up in the Royal valley of Seri Menanti, surrounded by rolling hills of lush vegetation, I spent a large part of my childhood outside in the palace grounds. My late father, the first post-independence King of Malaysia, was a keen sportsman and encouraged us to spend as much time outdoors as possible. In those days Malaysia was a natural playground. We didn't have to worry about crossing the road as cars were limited and really, development was still very slow. Everywhere you looked you were surrounded with greenery, plants, plants and more plants.

Today we are not so lucky. Malaysia, in particular Kuala Lumpur, has grown tremendously. It is barely recognisable from my earlier days. My two youngest children cannot play as I used to with the same absolute abandonment. Everywhere you look roads crisscross each other and cars run helter skelter. As such, it is vital in today's modern society that we maintain some areas which development cannot touch.

The parks within Kuala Lumpur and its surrounds provide such a perfect environment. Many a time I have enjoyed my early morning walks in The Lake Garden near my house while further afield in our administrative capital of Putrajaya a new development is unfolding, the Putrajaya Botanical Garden.

Whilst still in development, the first phase of this botanical garden has been opened to the public. It provides an incredible retreat for those in the public service and the public alike. Endless winding paths lead you through a multitude of gardens from Moroccan themed through African to Tropical. Here you will find the whole host of flora which is our national natural heritage. The colour and diversity of our indigenous plants played out in full Technicolor.

I am so grateful that our government has the foresight to understand the importance of such gardens and tropical wonderlands. Without them our children would not be able to take pleasure from these bounties of nature and be able to play, maybe not in the same way, as I did as a child.

**H.H. PRINCE ABDULLAH**
FOUNDER, MELEWAR GROUP BHD
KUALA LUMPUR, MALAYSIA

# SABAH AGRICULTURE PARK (TAMAN PERTANIAN SABAH)

## TENOM, SABAH  MALAYSIA

OPENED IN 2000, THIS PARK OF 500 SPRAWLING HECTARES LIES WITHIN THE 1,500 HA OF THE AGRICULTURAL RESEARCH STATION ON BORNEO. ITS INCREDIBLY RICH BIODIVERSITY INCLUDES A MULTITUDE OF INDIGENOUS AS WELL AS INTRODUCED PLANTS SPECIES SET AGAINST THE BACKDROP OF THE CROCKER RANGE (THE LONGEST IN THE COUNTRY) AND PANORAMIC LAKES. AS A RESEARCH INSTITUTE, IT IS ALSO A CONSERVATION CENTRE OF THE NATIVE ORCHIDS OF BORNEO AND ITS PROGRAMMES EDUCATE IN NATURE CONSERVATION AND THE PRESERVATION OF PRIMARY RAINFOREST. THE GROUNDS THEMSELVES RANGE FROM CULTIVATED GARDENS TO SPRAWLING JUNGLE, RESEARCH CENTRES AND LAKES. THERE ARE 21 ORNAMENTAL GARDENS INCLUDING THE BOUGAINVILLEA COURT, HIBISCUS GARDEN, ORIENTAL GARDEN AND CACTUS GARDEN. AGRICULTURE IS HERALDED THROUGH THE LIVING CROP MUSEUM, DEMONSTRATION FARMS AND A BEE CENTRE AMONGST OTHERS. VISITORS ARE INVITED TO HIKE THROUGH THE NUMEROUS JUNGLE TRAILS AND A VARIETY OF ACTIVITIES ARE AVAILABLE.

The world-class Sabah Agriculture Park is located in a beautiful valley near Tenom, and is a three hour drive from the state capital Kota Kinabalu over the Crocker Range and down through the scenic Keningau Valley to the Tenom Valley.

This State Park was carefully chosen, since at 200 metres altitude it receives cool night breezes from the mountains, and lies in a rain-shadow belt. The drier climate and cool night temperature make it one of a few places in Sabah, where many lowland tropical and semi-tropical flowering trees and shrubs flower profusely.

For this part of South East Asia, it is unique for containing over 30 horticultural gardens and demonstration farms reflecting the many activities of its custodian, the Sabah Ministry of Agriculture and Food Industries. Fisheries and Animal Husbandry are also incorporated, and the Park is a centre for information, education and recreation as well as a tourist attraction.

The Park has access to a 200 hectare reserve to allow for future development, and is integrated with an Agricultural Research Centre: nearly 100 hectares have been developed so far. Highlights for most visitors are the gardens that show off plant groups from around the world and their differing uses. These compact gardens are landscaped, with information panels provided, and most of the plants are labelled.

Of special interest, and a major attraction is the landscaped Hybrid Orchid Garden which displays a riot of different coloured flowers, and the Borneo Native Orchid Centre (Tenom Orchid Centre), with a Conservation Collection located by a forest stream. This centre includes nearly 400 native orchid species of which the slipper orchids of Borneo such as *Paphiopedilum rothschildianum* are among the most beautiful in the world and endemic to Sabah.

The Centre has an information booth, and also has the first successfully grafted Rafflesia plant, a parasite on a vine, with the largest flowers in the world, which is of particular significance for conservation.

The other gardens form a mosaic planted along paths that surprise the visitor, as he enters from one garden into the next. Bougainvillea, Hibiscus. Gingers, Heliconia, Ixoras, Aroids, flowering shrubs, Hoyas and Pitcher plants as well as arid land plants such as Cacti, provide a huge variety of flora for the public to view.

Other gardens provide a collection of ideas for landscaping suburban and town gardens, including an oriental style garden.

The central area of the Park, with its entrance and car parks, is an open park concept with three lakes, collections of flowering trees and water plants with fishing and cycling activities available. One lake fronts a farm-animal zoo, another, dotted with its islands, is utilised for camping and boating. Also in this area are hostels and a restaurant, while chalets are being developed.

Of special interest is the 4 hectare Living Museum of Crop Plants, arranged in sections to display a whole range of economic plants from around the world, in particular tropical fruit and nut trees including many native Borneo species.

Other popular sections are the tropical spices, culinary herbs, beverage crops, tropical vegetables, medicinal plants, fibre producing species, industrial crops, and ethno-botanical plants used by the rural communities. This has proved to be one of the most interesting and popular parts of the Park, which can absorb visitors for hours.

Another unique educational feature is the Garden of Evolution, tracing the evolution of plants from the beginning of time, with many amazing species used as examples.

Other notable projects are two of several 5-hectare demonstration farms, with more to be developed. One is planted with cash crops and fruits as a basis for Apiculture and Beekeeping, as Sabah is a World Centre of diversity for honey bees with five out of nine species. A special Bee Museum is located on this farm with a landscaped 'English' style border garden with colourful tropical plants that bees utilise. The other is a Self Sufficiency farm growing nearly everything that a family would need in life including a range of fruits, vegetables, grain crops, fibre crops, nuts, spices, a whole range of beverages, medicinal and even perfume plants, and insecticidal plants. Fish ponds, sago and peach, palms and animal farming are incorporated.

In the hill area of the Park, six kilometres of forest trails, with a canopy walkway, lead you to an area set aside for Agro-forestry Projects, Steep-land Agricultural Technology, demonstration rubber and deer farm, and several Rattan, Forestry and Forest plantation plots.

The Park is very popular during school holidays, with a host of activities on offer including fishing, boating and cycling, and forest walks. Future development may include mountain bike and horse riding trails.

The 'Trail of Discovery' for all visitors from the city dweller, the farmer or student using its educational facilities, its plant conservation activities, to its inspiration for garden landscaping makes the Park unique.

Above all, it is an agricultural park experience at its best in The Land Below The Wind, Sabah, Malaysian Borneo in the heart of the floristically rich eco-region of Malesia.

**TENGKU ZAINAL ADLIN, PH.D**
CHAIRMAN, SABAH TOURISM BOARD
KOTA KINABALU, SABAH

# SINGAPORE BOTANIC GARDENS
## SINGAPORE

ESTABLISHED IN 1859, THESE 19TH CENTURY TROPICAL BOTANIC GARDENS WERE ORIGINALLY LAID OUT AS A LEISURE GARDEN AND ORNAMENTAL PARK BY THE SINGAPORE HORTICULTURAL SOCIETY. IN 1874 THE GARDENS WERE HANDED OVER TO THE GOVERNMENT AND NOW FALL UNDER THE PURVIEW OF THE NATIONAL PARKS BOARD. IN 1936 THE LATE PROFESSOR R.E. HOLTTUM, THEN DIRECTOR OF THE BOTANIC GARDENS, CREATED THE SINGAPORE GARDENING SOCIETY. THE BOTANIC GARDENS MAINTAINED STRONG LINKS WITH THE SOCIETY UNTIL WELL AFTER THE SECOND WORLD WAR AND TODAY THE SOCIETY ACTIVELY PARTICIPATES IN VARIOUS HORTICULTURAL EVENTS ORGANISED BY THE NATIONAL PARKS BOARD. COVERING MORE THAN 63 HECTARES, THE GARDENS TODAY ARE A KEY CIVIC AND COMMUNITY RECREATIONAL PARK, AN IMPORTANT TOURIST DESTINATION AND A LEADING TROPICAL AND HORTICULTURAL INSTITUTION. HISTORICALLY, THEY HAVE PLAYED AN IMPORTANT ROLE IN THE INTRODUCTION AND PROMOTION OF MANY PLANTS OF ECONOMIC VALUE IN SOUTH EAST ASIA, INCLUDING THE PARA RUBBER TREE. THEIR COLLECTION OF MORE THAN 10, 000 TYPES OF PLANTS INCLUDES THE REGION'S MOST SIGNIFICANT LIVING COLLECTION OF DOCUMENTED PALMS, ORCHIDS, CYCADS AND GINGERS THEY ARE ALSO AN IMPORTANT CENTRE FOR TROPICAL BOTANICAL AND HORTICULTURAL RESEARCH, EDUCATION AND CONSERVATION.

In 1822, less than three years after planting the British flag, Stamford Raffles planted a Botanical Garden. It was re-established at its present site in 1859 by an agri-horticultural society on land still infested with tigers. From 1875 till the independence of Singapore, it was managed as one of the many British Colonial Gardens that girdled the globe. Its mission was botanical exploration, documentation, experimentation and research.

The first Director of the Gardens, Henry Nicholas Ridley (1888-1912), was the visionary who tirelessly experimented with and persuaded landowners to grow rubber, *Hevea brasiliensis*. By 1917, the Gardens had distributed over seven million rubber seeds and by 1920 Malaya was producing 50% of the world's rubber, and Singapore was the rubber capital of the world.

Over the following decades, the Botanic Gardens assumed a leading role in botanical research in the region. It pioneered the orchid-breeding programme in 1928, which continues to thrive today. The Gardens also spearheaded national 'greening' efforts from the 1960s, and established a School of Ornamental Horticulture to train workers needed to implement and maintain the Garden City.

In 1990, the Gardens re-established its roles and goals, and forged a new vision as a botanical institution. It re-developed research and educational outreach programmes, greatly expanded botanical collections and created new plant displays. Its National Orchid Garden, Ginger Garden, the Palm Valley, Evolution Garden and Children's Garden are highly regarded. Visitor amenities were built and new services introduced.

The Botany Centre, which was opened in 2006, houses the heart and soul of the Botanic Gardens, its research and educational facilities. These include the herbarium, laboratories, library, and function spaces. They play a crucial role in furthering the Gardens' position as a leading tropical botanic garden and institution, and its development as a knowledge hub for the region.

Amidst the many changes in the Singapore urbanscape over time, the Gardens remain a constant. Its verdant landscapes and giant trees have captured the imagination and loyalty of its visitors, both local and foreign. They are embedded in their memories giving them a sense of place. Visits now number over three million a year.

**MRS CHRISTINA ONG**
CHAIRMAN, NATIONAL PARKS BOARD
SINGAPORE

# NATIONAL ORCHID GARDEN, SINGAPORE BOTANIC GARDENS
## SINGAPORE

LOCATED IN THE SINGAPORE BOTANIC GARDENS, THE NATIONAL ORCHID GARDEN IS THE HOME OF MORE THAN 1, 000 SPECIES AND 2, 000 ORCHID HYBRIDS. THE INCREDIBLE DIVERSITY, RICHNESS AND BEAUTY OF THESE ORCHIDS MAKES THIS THE LARGEST DISPLAY OF TROPICAL ORCHIDS IN THE WORLD AND A TESTAMENT TO THE ORCHID BREEDING PROGRAMME INTRODUCED TO THE GARDENS IN 1928. MOST OF THE ORCHIDS IN TODAY'S GARDEN HAVE BEEN "HANDCRAFTED" BY THE HORTICULTURAL STAFF IN THE GARDENS AND ARE INDEED A LABOUR OF LOVE DEDICATED TO CAPTURING THE FINEST IN ANY HYBRID CROSS. THE ORCHID GARDEN ITSELF ALSO COMPRISES A MIST HOUSE, A COOL HOUSE AND ORCHIDARIUM AND A MAZE OF FLOWERING ORCHID PATHS AND HOUSES.

Cool tumbling water greets the visitor; high rocks with ferns and orchids, nature's oldest and most recent creations frame the waterfall at the entrance to the National Orchid Garden, Singapore's pride, and known by every traveller around the world. A sweeping path leads one upwards through shining golden showers of *Oncidiums*, orchids of the Andean foothills of the New World, that line our way and envelope us with wedding archways to give us joy and shade. At the summit of the little hill is the Old World, Burkill Hall, sometime British residence in the colonial days. Here distinguished visitors stayed and drank Gin Slings; now it is host to such honoured guests again, but nature's own, in the VIP Orchid Garden. Princes and prelates, prime ministers and presidents, rock stars and royalty all give their names to a palette of very special orchid hybrids raised in the Garden. There are arching scarlet *Renanthera*, Tyrian purple and purity pink-white *Dendrobium*, gently bowing golden *Spathoglottis*, and polychromic *Vanda*. Children recite their names, with the lilt of nursery rhymes: '*Renantanda, Bookchoonara, Kagawara* too, *Aranthera, Holltumara, Himoriara* who!?

In this little garden within a garden are orchids named to honour Prince Norodom Sihanouk, Princess Mikasa, Margaret Thatcher, and others who have passed through. All are hybrids bred and raised by the staff of the National Orchid Garden. As one moves back to the main garden one sees more of their handiwork with some of the 2,000 different hybrids and 1,200 species of orchids that are grown here.

A little shaded oasis, the mist house, is the display area for special plants that have come into flower behind the scenes. Here, Singaporeans and tourists alike marvel and, in modern style, click their Canons and their Nikons in homage to the fantastic blooms before strolling down among frangipani trees laden with curious *Bulbophyllum, Coelogyne, Dendrochilum* and names too weird to remember, and past herbaceous borders resplendent with massed *Dendrobium.* Here too is *Vanda* Miss Joaquim, the National Flower of Singapore, famous for a century and more.

This is a garden of magic, of surprises, and the best is left for last as one wends along an aerial pathway, with orchids on the slopes below, into a slender building of glass and steel. There is the roar of the giant waterfall descending into a deep gorge, trees that rise out of a canyon festooned with orchids from the cool mountains of the Himalayas of India, the Cordillera of Latin America, and the cloud forests beyond the upper reaches of the Yangtze gorges. The temperature drops ten degrees, and a cold mist envelops all in a fog so dense that the orchids disappear, and as quickly return. This is the new jewel of the Garden, a triumph of technology to sustain these orchids whose astonishing evolution, diversity, elegance and often strangeness, led the great botanist, John Lindley, to exclaim, in 1833: '*...for what sense can they have been formed unless to delight the sense of man, to gratify his eye by their gay colours and fantastic forms, and to show the inexhaustible fertility of that creative power which we recognise everywhere in nature.*' Here at the National Orchid Garden, they do just that.

**DR. HENRY OAKELEY**
PRESIDENT, ORCHID SOCIETY OF GREAT BRITAIN
KENT, UNITED KINGDOM

# KRANJI WAR CEMETERY
## KRANJI SINGAPORE

THIS 20TH CENTURY PERMANENT WAR CEMETERY COMMEMORATES THE COMMONWEALTH AND ALLIED SOLDIERS WHO DIED DURING THE BATTLE OF SINGAPORE AND THE JAPANESE OCCUPATION OF THE ISLAND (1942-1945) AND THOSE WHO DIED IN OTHER PARTS OF SOUTH EAST ASIA DURING THE WAR. THE SITE WAS ORIGINALLY A MILITARY CAMP WHICH, AFTER THE FALL OF THE ISLAND, BECAME A PRISONER-OF-WAR CAMP. TODAY'S CEMETERY WAS DEVELOPED OUT OF THE SMALL CEMETERY STARTED BY THE PRISONERS DURING THE WAR. THE SINGAPORE MEMORIAL WITHIN THE GROUNDS BEARS THE NAMES OF 24,000 COMMONWEALTH FORCES WAR CASUALTIES WHO HAVE NO KNOWN GRAVE. THE CEMETERY WAS DESIGNED TO LINK THE GARDENS OF HOME AND THE FIELDS WHERE THE SOLDIERS LAY, FLOWERS OF ENGLISH COTTAGE GARDENS ARE CLUSTERED ALONG THE LONG ROWS OF HEADSTONES AND VARY ACCORDING TO THE NATIONALITY OF THE SOLDIER WHO LIES THERE.

This unique and beautiful memorial park is sited on a gentle hilly slope that, at its highest point, rises four metres from road level. For more than sixty years it has distinguished itself as the only such large-scale war cemetery garden in Singapore, if not in South East Asia, dedicated to those who gave their lives in service of king and country. It is also unique for being a congregate of different memorials, parts (except the State Cemetery) that form a peaceful whole to mark a tragic moment in history.

Kranji War Cemetery was developed from a small cemetery started by prisoners in 1946 under the War Graves Service. It expanded to consist of the Singapore Memorial dedicated to remember over 24,000 names of casualties of Commonwealth land and air forces who had no known graves, or date of death, except for the fact of being confirmed by records as missing or captured. Many died during campaigns in Malaya or Indonesia or the infamous Death Railway.

Incorporated into Kranji was also the Singapore (Unmaintainable Graves) Memorial which accommodated 250 casualties with known graves from civil cemeteries that were unable to be maintained. Also remembered are 800 casualties mainly of the Indian forces who were cremated according to their religious rites; this is the Singapore Cremation Memorial. The Singapore Civil Hospital Grave Memorial is another component—here in the last hours of the battle of Singapore, civilians and servicemen were wounded and lost their lives and were buried in the former water tank of the hospital earlier built at Kranji, a spot consecrated by the Bishop and marked by a cross. In addition 69 Chinese servicemen are memorialised in the Chinese Memorial, another part of Kranji Memorial.

In total there are 64 burials of war dead from World War I and 4,394 plus 850 unknown from World War II. Altogether over 24,000 names are inscribed, the bulk of whom were unrecovered, missing in action: a tragic loss and a lesson for today.

The grounds peak at the hilltop which is crowned with a soaring structure, designed by Colin St. Clair Oakes, resembling a warship's conning tower, flanked on either side by a phalanx of 12 sheltered walls bearing inscriptions of the names of the fallen, for whom the fortunes of war denied proper burial. Contemplation benches are found in each of the 12 pavilions.

Kranji Memorial, as it is known locally, exudes a distinct formality on approach. Two shelter towers with stone lattice-work mark the formal entrance; one of them houses a visitor's book and a copy of *The War Dead of the Commonwealth 1914-1918 & 1939-1945* book, complete with the full list of names.

One is struck by the geometry of the layout of graves, markers, plazas, walls and posts, all climaxing in a main structure at the crest, most bearing names and noble commemorative lines. Interspersed in the scheme are plantings that soften the stony effect of granite, marble and concrete, rising from flower beds or sprouting from the earth.

A SOLDIER OF THE 1939-1945 WAR

As if unifying all of the structures is the spreading carpet of verdant grass. Kranji was one of the first venues for the mass-scale use of 'carpet grass' *(Zoysia tenuifolia)*, whose characteristic is a cushiony high-pile effect of minute green blades. Local visitors, particularly 'baby-boomers' growing up post-war in the 1950s and 1960s, undistracted by modern entertainment and television, will recall the pleasure of roaming barefoot in this park when brought there by their families.

Visitors continue. Many make the pilgrimage from the UK, Australia, New Zealand, France and India to remember loved ones who paid the ultimate price and perished either on the seas, in the air or on the ground.

Unrelated to war, the graves of two late presidents, Mr Yusof bin Ishak (1910-1970) and Dr Benjamin Henry Sheares (1907-1981) are sited in the State Cemetery, set away from the main Kranji Memorial reserved for heads-of-states and maintained by the National Environment Agency.

As a tropical garden, trees are markedly absent as if to leave nothing between these graves and the heavens above, save for the soaring winds of the north-east or south-west monsoon. In between, the carpet grass brings relief from the searing tropical heat during the hot season, yet the grounds remain perpetually dry after rainfall, the result of easy run-off aided by the gentle slopes and good drainage.

Among the few trees seen on the periphery of the grounds are the Angsana *(Pterocarpus indicus)*, Casuarina *(Casuarina equisetifolia)*, some Mango trees *(Mangifera indica)* and Raintrees *(Samanea saman)*, all of which offer seasonal inflorescences of sometimes fragrant blow-away flowers or succulent fruit. Two majestically tall clumps of the Sealing Wax Palm *(Cyrtostachys renda)* grace the plaza at the top of the hill while a less mature pair is planted beside the entrance towers at the bottom of the slope.

Low-level shrubs sprout from the earth in parallel formation lines as the gravestones. Mostly dwarf-sized, they include yellow Allamanda *(Allamanda cathartica)*, orange Cape Honeysuckle *(Tecomaria capensis)*, white and purple Lantanas *(Lantana camara)*, magenta roses *(Rosaceae family)*, yellow Peanut Flower *(Arachis pintoi)*, blue Butterfly Bush *(Clerodendrum ugandense)*, fire-cracker red miniature hibiscus (Hibiscus family), saffron yellow African daisies *(Gerbera jamesonii)* and Hippeastrum lilies that usually bloom at Easter. Charming little white and purple Asters punctuate the lines of flowering plants.

Orange Ixora *(Ixora sps.)* is used as dividers, as are the Duranta shrubs with bluish purple flowers and orange fruiting seeds. All are of the miniaturised varieties that provide neat colourful posies without usurping the sombre dignity of the gravestones.

Maintenance and plantings have been under the care of the Commonwealth War Graves Commission. Its Keeper Ling Cheng Lai lives in a charming cottage on the grounds.

Immaculate lawns and carefully tended floral touches complement the formality and dignity of the Kranji Memorial. Undoubtedly, a fitting tribute to valour—a noble garden of peace and calm, more than sixty years on, that belies the pain, suffering and sacrifice of so many who paid the highest price.

**AILEEN T. LAU**
EDITOR OF "ORIENTAL ART" & AUTHOR
SINGAPORE

THE AIR OVER ...
BUT TO WHOM ...
DENIED THE CUSTOMAR...
ACCORDED TO THEIR COMRADES IN DEA...

THEY DIED FOR ALL FREE MEN

# SINGAPORE ZOOLOGICAL GARDENS
## MANDAI LAKE  SINGAPORE

OPENED IN 1973 THESE ZOOLOGICAL GARDENS COVER SOME 28 HECTARES AND ARE WORLD RENOWNED. SET WITHIN A RAINFOREST, THE "OPEN CONCEPT" OF THE GARDENS AND ENCLOSURES SIMULATE THE NATURAL LANDSCAPE AND HABITAT THE ANIMALS ARE FOUND IN, AND RANGE FROM SAVANNAH GRASSES TO TROPICAL JUNGLE. ANIMALS ARE SEPARATED FROM VISITORS EITHER BY DRY OR WET MOATS WHICH ARE SOMETIMES CONCEALED BY VEGETATION GIVING THE IMPRESSION OF SEEING THE ANIMALS THEMSELVES IN THE "WILD"; ONLY IN CASES WITH PARTICULARLY DANGEROUS ANIMALS ARE THERE GLASS-FRONTED ENCLOSURES. HOUSING MORE THAN 300 ANIMAL SPECIES, THESE ZOOLOGICAL GARDENS CATER TO MORE THAN 1.4 MILLION VISITORS A YEAR AND HAVE WON MANY LOCAL AND INTERNATIONAL TOURISM AWARDS.

It's strange that in a man-made and silver city, one finds a small space that man, animals and nature are so close at hand that you can almost touch their very existence. This is where I contemplate life.

With the eternal elements of Air, Earth, Water and Fire in attendance, I watch as they interweave like threads on a complex tapestry. Emerald, turquoise, vermillion and ochre swirling together in the wind which at first, makes no sense and then, when all is quiet and all is clear, a life takes shape.

In this moment we acknowledge the Present—our mind is stilled, centred and aware.

The multitude of colours weave into a natural pattern, like that of coloured threads before weaving, taking form and alignment in this process. The wind beats a rhythm through the leaves like a loom. Tangles of thread which have no form are slowly and carefully guided through an expert hand, and through that, the formless becomes form.

This evolution of interdependence is the spirit of creation. In the unformed infinite of nature, possibilities are made for all created phenomena.

A branch lets go of a leaf—some see it as the end, but I see it as a new beginning. One that gives way to new leaf, and the fallen leaf gives back to the new generation by providing sustenance from the earth. Thus, the cycle of life is echoed, its constant change reminding us that this Impermanence is the Eternal Truth.

I look at the strong trunk of the local Mandai Rain Tree and I see strength and beauty in its mottled bark, yet will the Mandai Rain Tree wonder if it is ugly because of its imperfections, its disproportionate top, branches that are not symmetrical, leaves that pop out randomly? If beauty is in the eye of the beholder it is through our acceptance and understanding of Life's Imperfections, her ever-changing cycle, that beauty is realised once more.

A butterfly comes to rest near me. Its eyes can't see its own beauty and grace. It will only live for a month or less. Yet, it sees beyond its cloak of colours and short existence to live life to the fullest. Living a life according to its nature, oblivious of 'permanence'. This is the essence of the empty nature of our Self.

Nature has no agenda; it just has a purpose—to go on living, and in living, giving itself, and others, life and joy. Shouldn't that be what we aim to do?

**BENNY ONG**
DESIGNER
SINGAPORE

# BOGOR BOTANIC GARDENS (TAMAN SARI KEBUN RAYA)
## BOGOR, WEST JAVA INDONESIA

BUILT IN 1817 THIS IS INDONESIA'S FIRST AND FOREMOST BOTANIC GARDEN. COVERING 87 HECTARES, THESE GARDENS WERE CONVERTED FROM THE PALACE GROUNDS AND ARE SAID TO BE INSPIRED BY SIR STAMFORD RAFFLES, THEN GOVERNOR OF JAVA. WITH MORE THAN 14,000 SPECIMENS OF TREES AND SHRUBS OF MORE THAN 5,000 SPECIES, THE GARDEN IS NOW A LEADER IN RESEARCH IN AGRICULTURE, FORESTRY, ANIMAL HUSBANDRY AND FISHERY. COMPRISING BEAUTIFULLY MANICURED FORMAL GARDENS, PALM GARDENS, PONDS INCLUDING THE GIANT AMAZON WATER LILY POND, ARID ZONES INCLUDING THE DRY MEXICAN GARDEN, FLOWERING BEDS AND AN EXPANSIVE WILD ORCHID COLLECTION, THIS BOTANIC GARDEN IS TRULY A MICROCOSM OF THE FLORA AND FAUNA OF INDONESIA AND A LARGE PART OF THE WORLD. THE GARDEN IS ALSO AN IMPORTANT PART OF BOGOR CITY, PROVIDING NOT ONLY EMPLOYMENT BUT ALSO A LARGE RECREATIONAL AREA FOR LOCAL RESIDENTS, VISITORS FROM JAKARTA AND MANY TOURISTS.

Driving south 60 kilometres at Jagorawi Toll, we reach Bogor, a country town 500 metres above sea level, with a population of 4.2 million people. Right at the centre of Bogor is the famous Bogor Botanic Gardens which circles the centre of the town and is adjacent to the Bogor Presidential Palace. Bogor Botanic Gardens is the largest garden in Indonesia and was founded on the 18th of May 1817 by Prof. C.G.C. Reinwardt, a German Professor who was at that time representing the Dutch in the latest British occupation in Indonesia. The garden is renowned nationally and internationally as one of the first research centres for tropical plants in the world. For Indonesians it is a green oasis—a peaceful community centre and serves as a lung for the crowded town of Bogor by absorbing air pollution.

Stretching across 87 hectares, this vast garden is wonderfully landscaped with natural contour lines consisting of hillside, valley and plateau. It is divided by the rocky Ciliwung River whose clean currents gently flow onward through Jakarta to the Java Sea. The garden houses an enormous collection of flora comprising 218 families, 1,267 genus and 14,141 species which have been grown and propagated in the garden since it was developed 2 centuries ago. As an example, some of the most important export commodities of Indonesia are plants that were first introduced in the garden, such as palm, tea, chocolate, quinine, vanilla, rubber and many others that still find Bogor Botanic Gardens their home.

Since it was founded, the garden functions as a place for the acclimatisation of plants from other continents. The collection are "giant trees" more than a century old which truly look amazing. Today, some of these trees are rarely found in their natural habitat and are propagated and disseminated in the garden to avoid extinction. As such, the garden has become an important ex-situ conservation centre in Indonesia. The most important in the collection are palm, orchid, bamboo, wooden tree, medicinal plants and ornamental plants.

The garden provides a range of education programmes catering to everything from pre-school children through to university students and adults. The aim of these programmes is to promote concern and love for our environment, and educate visitors on the nature and diversity of plants, their uniqueness, values and benefits. Many students and researchers both local and international use the facilities and collections of the garden for research.

As a favoured tourist destination in Indonesia, the garden attracts a wealth of domestic and foreign tourists daily. The appeal of this botanic garden is twofold. Firstly the garden's extensive collection is beautifully arranged in accordance to botanic rules and secondly, the garden provides endless green scenery and vast open space for the visitors.

Among the substantial lawns there are tranquil ponds and lakes with water plants, including Lily and Padma family. These considerably add to the beauty of the garden. A truly romantic view can be found at dusk or when the dawn breaks while the grass is wet with dew. In the early morning, many people can be found relaxing and exercising in the garden accompanied by a symphony of birds singing, the gentle flow of the Ciliwung river, the warmth of the sun and the fresh breeze. It is such a healthy and luxurious but simple life that the garden offers: a precious gift for us that is the harmony between nature and the soul.

The beautiful Bogor Botanic Gardens is not the only one. There are many to visit on our journey through the Noble Botanic Gardens of Indonesia: The treasures of Cibodas Garden in West Java, Purwodadi Garden in East Java and Eka Karya Garden in Bali are waiting. These are our other green heritages, each one unique and special. But each one needs to be thought of, to be remembered and touched in order to exist.

**PROFESSOR DR. UMAR ANGGARA JENIE**
CHAIRMAN, INDONESIAN INSTITUTE OF SCIENCES
JAKARTA, INDONESIA

# TIRTAGANGGA

KARANGASEM, EAST BALI  INDONESIA

MEANING "HOLY WATER OF THE GANGES," TIRTAGANGGA IS KNOWN AS ONE OF THE WORLD'S MOST ROMANTIC GARDENS. BUILT IN 1946, THESE ROYAL WATERGARDENS WERE THE BRAINCHILD OF THE LAST RAJA OF KARANGASEM, ANAK AGUNG ANGLURAH KETUT KARANGASEM, AN ARCHITECT AND LECTURER. NOT ONLY DID HE DESIGN THE ENTIRE GARDEN, HE ALSO WORKED SIDE BY SIDE WITH THE LABOURERS DIGGING THE GROUND AND LAYING THE FOUNDATIONS. WHEN THE GARDENS WERE SEVERELY DESTROYED IN THE 1960'S BY A SERIES OF EARTHQUAKES AND VOLCANIC ERUPTIONS, THE RAJA SOUGHT TO REPAIR THESE WATERGARDENS DESPITE SEVERE MONETARY CONSTRAINTS. IT WAS HIS SON WHO IN 1979 EVENTUALLY OVERSAW THE REHABILITATION OF THESE GARDENS. SURROUNDED BY RICE PADI AND FED BY THE NATURAL SPRINGS OF REJASA, THE GARDEN IS RESPLENDENT WITH ITS 11 TIERED LOTUS FOUNTAIN, A MYRIAD OF REFLECTING AND SWIMMING POOLS THAT SURROUND THE WATER PALACE AND THE PRESIDING ANCIENT BANYAN TREE AND HOLY TEMPLE.

One late afternoon in 1999 I was strolling around Tirtagangga. The sun was very low as it was just before sunset, causing a surrealistic light in the sky which at the same time was reflected in the water in front of me. From the southeast corner I had an overall view of the park. The magnificent banyan tree on the other side of the park dominated the scene. Under this tree is the temple around the spring that continuously feeds the ponds in the park. Like meaningful islands in the middle of a meaningless sea of land, there are some places in the world, such as the setting of the Banyan tree, that are more serene than their surroundings. Most temples in Bali are built on such a spot.

While contemplating the scene I felt a strange attraction towards the tree. In front of my eyes it seemed to grow immensely in proportion and in vivacity. It captured my attention more and more until nothing else existed but the tree. Many voices, wordless but which I could understand, seemed not to come from inside of me but from within the tree.

At first the voices imparted a distressing vision of the park falling into disrepair: parts which were already in decline seemed at that moment to become even more desolate and deteriorated than they were in reality. The broken gutters and pathways, the overgrowing weeds, the rubbish that was lying around and floating everywhere, the television antenna that spoiled the view and everything else in the park that was ugly struck me increasingly in intensity until I was completely overwhelmed with feelings of agony and despair.

Then this sombre vision slowly changed, firstly to a neutral one, and then gradually becoming more appealing until it was ultimately one of splendour. One by one the ugly statutes disappeared or were replaced by noble masterpieces. Water started once more to pour from the fountains. Suddenly the barbed wire disappeared, replaced by birds and butterflies that settled on flowers which seemed gradually to sprout from the ground all around. Golden fishes started to fill the ponds.

The voices from the tree seemed like the cries from a thousands souls. The souls of those deceased, those still alive and those yet to be born; people who had enjoyed the park in the past, were enjoying it in the present and were yet to enjoy it in the future. It was almost like a chorus yearning to transform the sad vision into the one of splendour. Until that moment I had cared little about the park, taking its existence for granted. But from that moment on I was determined to respond to their yearning.

Although the Banyan tree was still just as magnificent, it seemed to lose its grip over me. Gradually I was able to shift my attention from the tree to my surroundings. In the faint light of the sunset, the park once more assumed its normal form.

In reality all of this happened in the space of a few seconds, but to me it was a long and overwhelming experience. Soon after this occurrence I realised that this splendorous vision has also been shared by others; people whose support up until this moment has been crucial in transforming this image into reality.

Although many may have thought that I was the same person who continued his walk from the southeast corner of the park that afternoon, I knew that the Banyan tree had thoroughly changed me.

**ANAK AGUNG GEDE DHARMA WIDOERE DJELANTIK**
CHAIRMAN, TIRTAGANGGA
GUODA, THE NETHERLANDS

# VILLA BEBEK
## SANUR, BALI INDONESIA

THE GROUNDS AND GARDEN OF VILLA BEBEK ARE WHOLLY OWNED AND INSPIRED BY ITS CREATOR, MADE WIJAYA, AN AUSTRALIAN LANDSCAPE ARCHITECT FORMERLY KNOWN AS MICHAEL WHITE. CREATED IN THE 1980'S VILLA BEBEK IS A WONDERFUL EXAMPLE OF CONTEMPORARY BALINESE LANDSCAPING COMBINING A TYPICAL BALINESE ARRANGEMENT OF COURTYARDS, WATER FEATURES WITH PLANTING THAT ACHIEVES A JUNGLE-LIKE EFFECT. LILY PONDS REFLECT THE PALMS FROM THE SURROUNDING PLANTATIONS. AMONGST THE WEALTH OF FLORA THERE ARE BOUGAINVILLEAS, PLUMERIAS, AND VARIOUS SHRUBS. THE SWIMMING POOL IS PLANTED WITH PALMS & SMALLER TREES AND HAS A PERGOLA CASCADING WITH FLOWERS. THROUGHOUT THE GARDEN YOU WILL FIND A HUGE ASSORTMENT OF OBJECT D'ART COLLECTED THROUGHOUT INDONESIA OR CREATED AND SCULPTED BY LOCAL ARTISANS.

The Villa Bebek was built in 1983 as a series of pavilions in a large coastal-palace garden. I say "coastal-palace" because the compact *brahmana* and *kstaria* 'mini-palaces' of Sanur and Kuta had a unique 'coastal' feel. These gardens featured white sand on the courtyard floor of temples and a use of dry heat-loving plants like the *Cordyline Australis*, the plumeria, the bougainvillea, crotons and ixora, Raphis palms, MacArthur palms, cane palms and Alexander palms (my favourite) which are all happy on the coast.

During my studies into the architecture and gardens of the palaces of South East Asia, I used the Villa Bebek as a testing ground for various mini-palace 'looks' and nooks—statuary and water gardens in particular. It is by no means a noble house—I am an irreverent Australian —but the gardens remain today, some 25 years later, as a sort of mini-museum of Balinese garden features.

Nearly all the mini-palace gardens which inspired the Villa Bebek have long since disappeared, replaced with manicured masterpieces of municipalia.

**MADE WIJAYA**
PRINCIPAL DESIGNER, PT WIJAYA TRIBWANA INTERNATIONAL
BALI, INDONESIA

# MAKILING BOTANIC GARDENS
### LOS BAÑOS, LAGUNA LUZON PHILIPPINES

MOUNT MAKILING IS AN INACTIVE VOLCANO RISING TO ABOUT 1,109 METRES ABOVE SEA LEVEL AND A POPULAR HIKING ZONE. THESE BOTANIC GARDENS ARE LOCATED ON THE LOWER NORTHERN SLOPES OF THE MOUNTAIN AND WERE ESTABLISHED IN 1963 BY THE LATE PRESIDENT MACAPAGAL. WITH MORE THAN 2,000 SPECIES OF PLANT, THEY ARE ONE OF THE KEY ECO-TOURISM SITES IN THE PHILIPPINES. DEDICATED TO EDUCATION AND UNDERSTANDING ALL FORMS OF HORTICULTURE, THE BOTANIC GARDENS ARE ATTACHED TO THE COLLEGE OF FORESTRY AND NATURAL RESOURCES, UNIVERSITY OF PHILIPPINES AND ARE AN IMPORTANT OUTDOOR LABORATORY FOR THE ADVANCEMENT OF SCIENTIFIC KNOWLEDGE ON RAINFOREST ECOLOGY AND BIODIVERSITY CONSERVATION. THE MOUNTAIN ITSELF HAS ALWAYS BEEN SURROUNDED BY MYSTICISM; SOME SAY IT IS SHAPED IN THE FORM OF A RECLINING WOMAN. LEGEND SAYS THAT IT IS THE PROFILE OF THE SLEEPING MARIA MAKILING, A MYTHICAL GODDESS WHO LIVES IN THE MOUNTAIN AND PROTECTS RESIDENTS AND TRAVELERS FROM HARM.

The Philippine archipelago is made up of 7,100 verdant islands and it is biodiversity that defines the natural interior and the waters that surround each one. To a greater or lesser extent, this wealth is now eroded by pressures of an expanding population and encroaching urbanisation. These threats appeared in the last century, but mitigation, by way of forest conservation and a park system, came early in the 20th century.

Under American colonialism a Bureau of Forestry was established and the first forest reserve was established on the slopes of a long dormant, kilometre-high volcano—Mt. Makiling—63 kilometres south of the capital Manila. Governor General William Cameron Forbes signed the proclamation designating 3,800 hectares of primary forest as a reserve in 1910. Two years earlier the colonial government had established a rural campus of the fledgling University of the Philippines in Los Baños town at the foot of the mountain.

The town and mountain were already famous destinations for Spanish officials and travellers from Manila, along with adventurers from overseas, as early as the 17th century. The attractions were the hot springs and the baths that were established for their recuperative powers; hence the name Los Baños. In 1671, Franciscan missionaries built a church attached to a hospital. In the mid-nineteenth century a palace was added to the complex and served as the residence of the Capitan General. Subsequently, the palace was used as a hospital. This historical building has been conserved to this day as the Agua Santa Resort.

The other attractions were the flora and fauna. A species of the fabled Rafflesia was found in Makiling; also wild orchids and an amazing array of ferns and stories of this botanic treasure trove reached Spain and Europe. This forest ecosystem had also made it a prime habitat for a diverse range of fauna, and as such, a prime hunting site popular up to the early 20th Century. It was only prohibited after a proclamation issued by Forbes' successor, Francis Burton Harrison, in 1920 changing the Makiling Forest Reserve to a National Botanic Garden.

Harrison also appointed a committee to make a study and draft plans for the development of the botanic gardens. To further protect the site he issued a supporting executive order to prohibit "hunting, shooting, trapping, capture, injury (to) or destroying wild birds and animals within the Makiling National Botanical Garden." The exception was for the gathering and study of specimens by the different colleges in the university below. The institution was starting to play a key role in the area's conservation; a role that continues to this day.

Under subsequent governors-general, Makiling's area was sadly reduced by hundreds of hectares. This was to be rectified only in the 1930s as the Philippines transitioned into a commonwealth government led by Filipinos; a prelude to full independence.

President Manuel L. Quezon was the first commonwealth president. He was an ardent advocate of the great outdoors and the benefits of national parks for public leisure and enjoyment. Quezon wanted to replicate the success of the American national park system. He retained the services of an American landscape architect—Louis P. Croft. Croft had worked for the National Parks in the early 1930s and was tasked with undertaking a survey of the archipelago to determine the best areas to be included in a national park system.

Makiling was part of the study and records show that during Quezon's term (1935-1941) 21 parks were added to the system and the land area for Makiling was expanded. Unfortunately Croft's study and recommendations were lost in the Second World War when he was incarcerated in a Japanese internment camp in Manila. His post-war legacy was the establishment of the Bataan National Park with an area of 31,000 hectares.

In 1963 President Carlos P. Garcia issued a proclamation transferring the administration of the park to the UP College of Forestry "for forest education and research purposes, subject to the condition that the park shall be conserved and reserved as a national park." The area is now designated as the Makiling Forest Reserve, but is still widely known as the Makiling Botanic Gardens.

With local tourism on the rise in the 1960's, the government decided to develop a number of urban and national parks. It created the National Parks Development Committee (later attached to the Department of Tourism) tasked with managing key public parks—the Rizal Park in central Manila, two more small urban pocket parks and a six hectare recreational facility in the middle of the Makiling Botanic Gardens—the *Pook ni Maria Makiling*.

This facility is the main site for visitors to the gardens and the mountain. Cabañas, an Olympic-sized swimming pool, aviary and picnic areas were built in the early 1970s. The *'Pook'* (Filipino for place) is named after the resident spirit of the mountain—Maria Makiling. *Makiling* is Filipino for crooked—descriptive of the mountain's three peaks—which look like a silhouette of a woman. She is one of the most famous *diwata* (nymph) in Philippine mythology. Local legends tell the story of this *diwata*, who never failed to help local villagers by bringing good fortune, falling in love with a mortal man and being spurned. This led to her disappearing into the mountain never to be seen again or offering intercession in times of need. Maria Makiling (and other 'Marias' in other mountains in the Philippines) symbolizes nature's capacity to nurture man and the importance of treating her bounty with respect.

Today Makiling remains one of the most visited of national parks in the Philippines. However it, and the other national parks in the Philippines, is dangerously threatened by illegal logging, swidden agriculture, informal settlements, pollution and encroaching urbanisation at its various sites.

These threats are compounded by the metropolitan sprawl from the capital and a regional population of over fifteen million which has reached well past its green borders. Tract housing, resorts and golf courses, pollution and an expanding highway infrastructure are choking the mountain to death. Maria Makiling may show up one day soon to once again remind us to rekindle our fragile relationship with her or suffer the consequences.

**PROFESSOR PAULO ALCAZAREN**
COLLEGE OF ARCHITECTURE, UNIVERSITY OF PHILIPPINES
MANILA, PHILIPPINES

# MALACAÑAN PALACE GROUNDS

MALACAÑAN PALACE, MANILA  PHILIPPINES

THE OFFICIAL RESIDENCE OF THE PRESIDENT OF THE PHILIPPINES, MALACAÑAN PALACE IS LOCATED ALONG THE SOUTH BANK OF THE PASIG RIVER IN MANILA. ORIGINALLY BUILT IN 1802 AS A SUMMER HOME FOR A SPANISH ARISTOCRAT, THE BUILDING WAS LATER BOUGHT BY THE STATE AS A RESIDENCE FOR THE GOVERNORS-GENERAL. IT WAS ONLY IN 1935 THAT IT FIRST BECAME USED AS THE PRESIDENTIAL PALACE. IN THE 1960'S THE FIRST LADY, MRS MACAPAGAL DEDICATED MUCH OF HER TIME TO CLEANING UP THE PALACE AND RESTORING AND RESCUING THE PALACE GROUNDS, THE HOUSE ZOO AND THE PARK ACROSS THE RIVER WITH WHAT WOULD BE CONSIDERED A MODEST BUDGET. ITS FORMAL LAWNS AND CLIPPED TOPIARY CONTRAST PERFECTLY WITH THE LUSH PALM AND TROPICAL VEGETATION WITHIN IT.

Metropolitan Manila is one of the largest and most densely populated mega-cities in South East Asia, full of the bustle, colour and enthusiasm for which Filipinos are famous. Amidst the heat and commotion it is easy to forget that the capital of the Philippines was once fabled for its breathtaking natural setting, with the curve of Manila Bay to the west where the sun sets and dazzles, to the great lake Laguna de Ba'i and the mountains of the Sierra Madre in the east. In between were a multitude of waterways lacing around the stately and expansive Pasig River, at the mouth of which—where the waters of the lake were finally emptied into the bay and the South China Sea beyond—the heart of Manila stands.

All the old accounts and chronicles speak of a luxuriant and abundant tropical paradise, in the midst of which country houses were erected during Spanish colonial times. The best of these vied for frontage along the wide reaches of the Pasig, including that established in the 1750s by Luís Rocha, a merchant who converted "sixteen hectares of swampland into one large well-planned garden as a lovely setting for his mansion." This was the genesis of the property that would later be known as Malacañan Palace (or simply Malacañang): it would serve as the summer home of the Spanish governors-general of the Philippines from 1847, the residence of the Spanish and then American governors-general from 1863, and then the seat of the President of the Philippines from 1935 to the present.

Across all these periods, the grounds of the Palace and their location along the river have been considered the chief glories of the property, but it was in the late 1930s, under the Palace's first official Filipino resident, President Manuel L. Quezon of the Commonwealth of the Philippines, when the grounds of Malacañang arrived at more or less their present configuration and appearance. The most well-known part of the grounds is the main garden fronting the main façade of the Palace, the principle features of which include a magnificent Art Deco fountain with four caryatids in traditional Filipino dress or *balintawak*, a pair of Spanish bronze cannon from the 1860s bearing the cipher of Isabel II which flanks the archway of the beautiful trellis leading to the riverside promenade and, most famously, Mr. Brown—a massive strangler plant which forms what is known locally as a Balete tree.

The grounds have an extensive history as visitors have long admired their beauty. In 1898, Ramon Reyes Lala in his book The *Philippine Islands* recorded that the "The garden is famed for its luxuriance. Here grow, in a rich profusion, coconuts, bananas, lemons, mangoes and a wealth of flowers: the white champaca, the yellow *ilang-ilang* with its exquisite perfume, gigantic orchids, and a thousand other blooms." Efforts in the 1920s and 1930s were devoted to collecting specimens representative of all Philippine flora from the tallest hardwood trees to ferns and orchids.

During the Second World War, the grounds suffered unfortunate neglect and then, after the liberation of the capital by Allied forces in February, 1945, complete devastation. Every inch of open space was cleared and converted into barracks, way stations, makeshift government offices, and a relief centre. The gardens, shorn of almost everything but the grand old trees of colonial times, would not recover their glory for many years as post-war rehabilitation of the gardens was sporadic until one First Lady took it in hand to devote the required attention. This was my grandmother, Evangelina Macapagal, wife of my grandfather, Diosdado Macapagal, who was President of the Philippines from 1961 to 1965. Strongly concerned with the beautification of public spaces and gardens, Mrs. Macapagal refurbished the grounds, created a rose garden by the river adjacent to the Palace and installed noteworthy sculpture.

My mother, President Gloria Macapagal-Arroyo, was a young teenager during these years and remembers well how hard her mother worked to achieve the right balance between elegance and practicality, comfort and simplicity, privacy and public openness, while maintaining a sense of expansive space. She made sure that no further structures or buildings were constructed at the expense of space, gardens and trees.

It was also from my grandmother that my mother and the rest of us learned to appreciate the role and responsibility of stewardship, that one must keep the beauty and dignity of the Palace and its gardens for the national patrimony.

Many changes took place after the Macapagal presidency and during the administration of Ferdinand Marcos, which lasted over twenty years from 1965 to 1986. The Palace itself, a unique but somehow harmonious agglomeration of over two centuries of additions and enlargements, was in 1979 almost wholly demolished and rebuilt as a modern, larger structure, and in the early 1980s parts of the grounds and the wider Palace complex fell into neglect or were given over to security facilities. By this time too, the public were largely barred from entering Malacañang.

After the EDSA People Power Revolution in 1986, the Palace was opened again to the people and the effort to restore the grounds to their full glory commenced. A significant contribution was made through the mid-1990s by First Lady Amelita Ramos, an enthusiastic gardener who today maintains her own nursery stocked with a marvelous variety of plants in a scenic location south of Manila.

For our part, having had the privilege of residing at the Palace since 2001, the sense of open space and expansive greenery is always easy to take pleasure in. Among the family, it is my mother who is most concerned with the state and appearance of the grounds, which she holds to be in a certain sense sacred. She always takes the opportunity to walk around, pointing out some improvement that can be made and always favouring more garden rather than less. Tending to the physical needs of the palace is her form of relaxation, and her homage to my grandmother's tenets on simple yet dignified stewardship.

For my mother and our family, it is only with patience, care, sustained effort and faith that results can be achieved which Filipinos now and into the future can take pride in and deservedly enjoy. So it is with respect to the great multitude of other, vastly larger, responsibilities of the President of the Philippines, as with the wonderful and storied gardens of Malacañan Palace.

**EVANGELINA LOURDES "LULI" M.ARROYO**
REGIONAL POLICY OFFICER, WORLD WIDE FUND FOR NATURE
MANILA, PHILIPPINES

EAST ASIA

CHINA   SOUTH KOREA   JAPAN

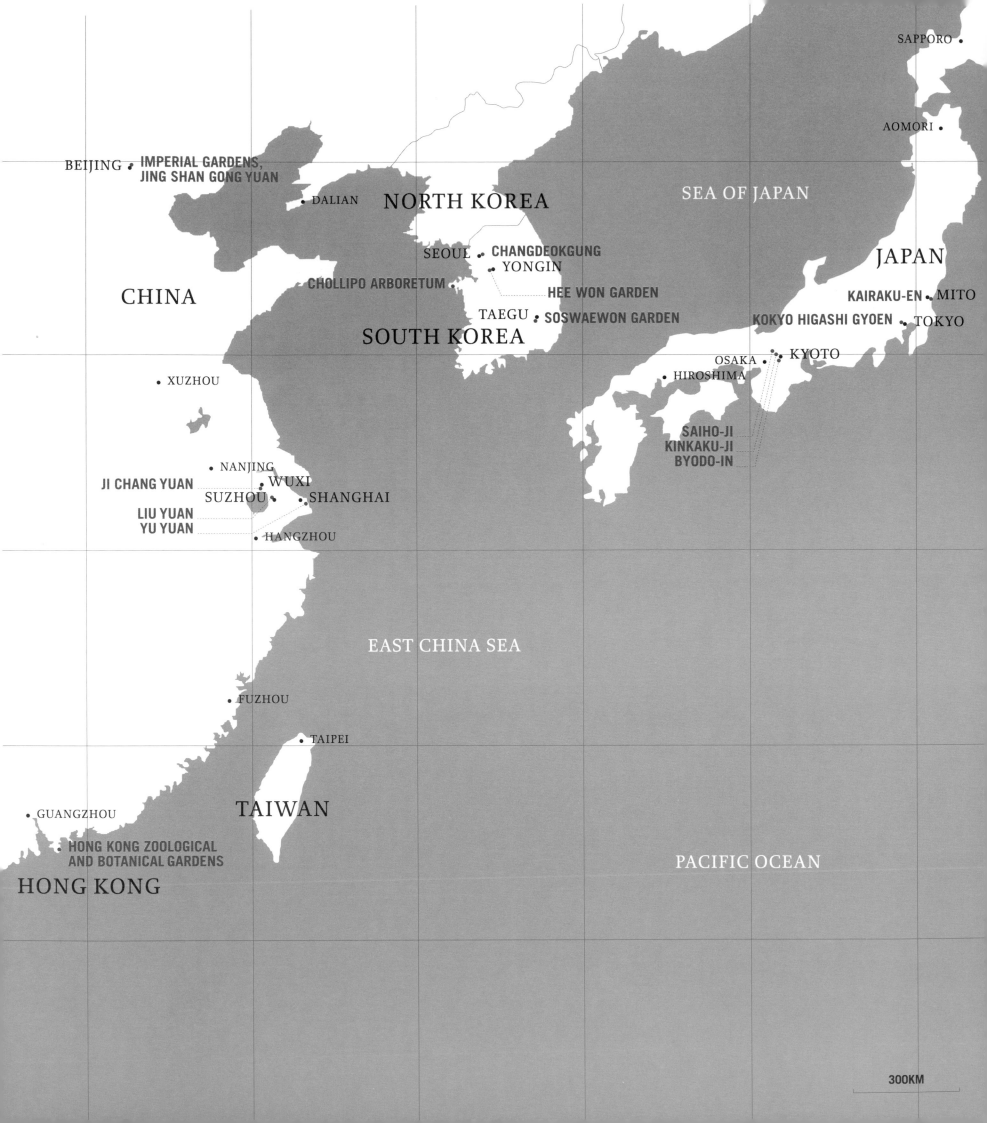

SAPPORO •

AOMORI •

BEIJING • **IMPERIAL GARDENS,
JING SHAN GONG YUAN**

• DALIAN NORTH KOREA

SEA OF JAPAN

JAPAN

CHINA

SEOUL • **CHANGDEOKGUNG**
• **YONGIN**

CHOLLIPO ARBORETUM •

**HEE WON GARDEN**

**KAIRAKU-EN** • MITO

**KOKYO HIGASHI GYOEN**

TAEGU • **SOSWAEWON GARDEN**

**TOKYO**

SOUTH KOREA

OSAKA •

**KYOTO**

• XUZHOU

• HIROSHIMA

**SAIHO-JI
KINKAKU-JI
BYODO-IN**

• NANJING

**JI CHANG YUAN**

• **WUXI**

SUZHOU •

• SHANGHAI

**LIU YUAN
YU YUAN**

• HANGZHOU

EAST CHINA SEA

• FUZHOU

• TAIPEI

• GUANGZHOU

TAIWAN

• **HONG KONG ZOOLOGICAL
AND BOTANICAL GARDENS**

PACIFIC OCEAN

HONG KONG

300KM

## THE EAST ASIAN GARDEN—CHINA, KOREA AND JAPAN

The major difference between European and Islamic gardens compared with Asian gardens is that the latter look upon water and miniature hills of rock and stone as seas and mountains. Among European gardens some, like the Villa Lante in Bagnaia in Italy, link cascades and the water surface at the bottom of the cascade with mountain streams and the sea; however, these are exceptional cases. Buckminster Fuller deduced that people who once lived in South East Asia migrated, along with their culture, towards the north along the great rivers at the end of the ice age. If his hunch is correct, it can be said that the memory of the great sea dwelling in the hearts of these people, was carried up to the north to inland China, contrary to the commonly believed route, and it has been passed down to us, the present inhabitants of East Asia, who also regard water in the garden as the sea. In this sense, this publication, which encompasses Asian gardens, is both interesting and meaningful as it reconfirms the link within the primitive memories of Asian people.

In East Asia, namely, China, Korea and Japan, the concept of sea and mountain has particular emphasis in their gardens. *Sakutei-Ki*, a textbook of garden and landscape design written in Japan at the end of the 11th century, describes the garden design by identifying the pond in the garden, the stream flowing into the pond and miniature hills and rocks dotting the pond as the sea, river and islands respectively. However, this is not a new concept founded in Japan, but one which has been around for a long time in China and Korea, countries with a longer history of garden culture than Japan. If the subject of gardens is explored on a very deep plane, it eventually reaches mythology, and thus the belief in the existence of such things as stones, rocks and water becomes pivotal. In Japan, for example, there is a belief in the worship of an abnormally huge rock, found on a sacred mountain. It is thought that this is the rock on which the god appears, although some people consider this semi-natural, semi-artificial rock arrangement to be the beginning of a garden. The origin of the garden is certainly closely linked with worship and this can be found in all cultural spheres. In this article, however, I would like to go further, and consider how people in 3 areas of East Asia created gardens as the spot for their pleasure and thoughts and as the ideal microcosmos.

Among the 3 areas of East Asia, China has the longest history of gardens. The oldest garden found in literature dates back to the 11th century B.C. It was the vast area where the Emperors enjoyed hunting and it had some structures for recreation and relaxation as well as a place of worship. Since then, Chinese Emperors of different dynasties, in succession, made huge gardens with complex designs boasting incredibly large expanses to reflect the Emperors' enormous power. Most of them have been lost now and the scale covering even a mountain and lake can only be seen in a few existing gardens such as the Yi He Yuan in Beijing, formed during the Qing Dynasty, and the Summer Palace in Chengde which was the Emperor's summer villa.

While these magnificent gardens were built by Emperors, wealthy people and men of letters had started designing their own gardens since the Tang Dynasty. Various elements contributing to the features of Chinese gardens were gradually developed by this move. The methodologies used in these gardens were at once incorporated in the imperial gardens. Such gardens created by the rich and scholarly came to maturity during the period of the Song Dynasty through to the Ming Dynasty. They centred in the Jiannan region at the lower reach of the Yangtze River, which has lush greenery, abundant water and a warm climate. Suzhou, Shanghai and Wuxi where the Liu Yuan, Yu Yuan and Ji Chang Yuan are located, as well as Hangzou, where large gardens consisting of villas and hills surround the Xi Hu lake, Yangzhou and Shaoxing are famous for their stately gardens. However, it is very rare to find these gardens in their original shape due to historical changes in China. Most of the gardens we can see nowadays were modified or altered during the Qing Dynasty or a later period.

One of the major features of gardens belonging to the villas of the literati is the large number of buildings within the garden. From the grand hall to the small and open pavilions, buildings of differing sizes are positioned in the large gardens created behind the villas. These buildings are connected with covered galleries in the main areas. The galleries are sometimes winding to represent a long road, and people had to walk down these galleries in a leisurely way as if actually walking on the road. In some parts of the garden, there are partition walls which have an opening of circular or other artistic shapes. A smaller inner garden is found on the other side of these walls and this structure is often repeated many times. The partition wall for this "garden within a garden" is painted white to gracefully reflect the shadows of plants and trees. These walls also have several openings with beautiful openwork (called *luochuang* in Chinese) so that light, wind and rain can flow through. This is an artful and sophisticated approach to offset the sense of being boxed in by the partitions.

Till now, people have been saying that Chinese gardens are the apotheosis of poetry and painting, meaning that gardens should be imbued with the poetic sentiments and atmosphere of a painting. In spite of its long history in garden and landscaping, the *Yuan Ye*, the first landscaping textbook, was compiled only in the 17th century. This might have been so because treatises on painting had been playing the main role as the authority on garden design. These treatises on painting state that we should depict the "ideal landscape of the mind", which is the retired and quiet utopia where the Taoist immortals live. Chinese men of letters found the perfect material to make such a landscape—rocks of bizarre appearance formed by the erosion of wind and water of the lake. This type of rock was named *Taihushi* after the lake in which they were produced and became an essential element of the gardens made by the literati. Sometimes a hill, made of this type of rock and soil, had a grotto, the residence of the Taoist immortal, in its inner part and an open pavilion *(ting)* built at the hilltop vantage point. This combination became popular in Europe during the period of Orientalism and this influence can be seen in many European gardens which have a pagoda. "Find large in small, and find substance within emptiness" is also popularly quoted of Chinese gardens. Based on such a concept, garden designers would have imagined a rugged mountain and an endless ocean.

Like China, the history of Korean gardens began in the palaces of the ancient Emperors. The form of gardens first appeared in literature around the 5-6th century when the Korean peninsular was divided into 3 different kingdoms, Koguryo, Paekche and Silla. The writings mention that landscapers from Paekche came to Japan and created the courtly garden at the beginning of the 7th century. Similar remnants thought to be related to such a garden were also found in Japan. One existing remains of an ancient garden is the garden of the Donggung, or the East Palace, built by the Tongil Silla Dynasty in the late 7th century in Kyongju. This garden is called Anabji after the name of the pond. The remains have a contrasting structure with the straight line of the shore where the building stood and a natural curved line at the hillside. Square-shaped ponds were also popular in the gardens of the palaces in the Yi Dynasty at a later period. The Anabji pond has 3 small islands, symbols of legendary sacred mountains. This shows us that the Chinese idea of supernatural beings, including Taoist immortals, was passed from China to Korea. The Biwon or the Secret Garden in the Changdeok Palace of the Yi Dynasty is introduced in this publication. This garden has a Chinese influence, yet also possesses a unique feature of Korea which focuses less on its artificial flavour and more with the blending in with nature.

It is usually difficult for Imperial structures to rid themselves of formal constraints, but gardens made by the Korean literati are interesting in the point that the ideal landscape for the Korean people is expressed without restraint. The Soswaewon introduced in this publication is a good example. This garden was made by a literary man who was able to build a successful career as a young bureaucrat but, in the midst of political turmoil, was forced to give up his career and lead the life of a scholar in his hometown. A stream flows on the slope located in the centre of the garden and several open buildings are individually placed along the stream. This scenery is in perfect harmony with nature, with no boundary between artificiality and nature and no contrast between garden and outside environment. During this era, there were many gardens built by the literati. The "far from the madding crowd" ambience of these gardens and their peaceful harmony with great nature is fascinating.

As mentioned earlier, Japanese gardens were first developed and influenced by Korea. In the 8th century, methodologies using the structure of natural rocks—influence of the Tang Dynasty—and expressing the beach with pebbles *(suhama)* were seen. Since then, garden styles unique to Japan have been developed. It is clear that the present basic landscape of Japanese gardens were established during the Heian era. This is indicated by the fact that landscapes which very often use natural curves based on asymmetrical structures are described in detail in the abovementioned *Sakutei-Ki*. This literary work also describes that gardens should be created based on the natural appearance of mountains and sea. As can be seen from this description, Japanese garden landscapes are a reflection of the mountains and sea of the area where the garden is located. In any part of the world, the garden has a structure close to the surrounding landscape. In China, too, the complex rock structures of Chinese gardens are a replica of famous mountains of different areas such as Huang Shan. Meanwhile, additional elements were incorporated into Japanese gardens through several major historical changes. First of these is the creation of the Karesansui garden where abstract form is created using pebbles, stones, rocks and white sand alone without the use of plants. It is thought that the method of appreciating miniature artistic landscapes created on just a plate of stones arranged on white sand, inspired the Karesansui style. The Karesansui garden has a background of Zen thinking and thus this type of garden was usually formed in Zen temples. In China, too, there are some gardens whose landscape design comprises just stones or rocks on the surface embedded with pebbles and a kind of tile *(zhuan)*. However, the Karesansui of Japan seeks abstract shapes more deeply than Chinese gardens.

In addition, the world of the tea ceremony *(cha-no-yu)* added some new elements which are now regarded as essential to the Japanese garden. Such elements, stepping stones *(tobi-ishi)* and stone lantern *(ishidohroh)*, appeared in the *rogi* pathway to the tea ceremony room. Furthermore, the method of large-scale trimming or *ohkarikomi*, which conveys the notion of mass from the smooth surface of trimmed trees, became established and popular at a later period. This method is now accepted as a feature of Japanese gardens, while such large-scale trimming of trees cannot be seen in Chinese or Korean traditional gardens. Considering the fact that topiary was recognized as a trendy art style in Europe at the time when large-scale trimming became popular in Japan and that European culture was introduced to Japan by European missionaries at around the same time, it is possible to assume that the topiary method came into Japan from Europe. Apart from this, the method of borrowed scenery or *shakkei* was very often used in large gardens to incorporate scenery outside the garden into the landscape within the garden, especially in the Edo Period. As seen in the abovementioned history, Japanese gardens have been developed through incorporation of new, additional elements created at different periods. However, the phenomenon that new style supersedes old, which can often be seen in Europe, has never happened in Japan. Japanese culture has been developed by adding and incorporating new elements while maintaining its fundamental character. Needless to say, restraint and sophistication have been always required for Japan's superlative gardens. It is also notable that gardens created after the time of *Sakutei-Ki* are still intact today and maintain their original shape without major modification.

**PROFESSOR TADASHI YOKOYAMA**
PRESIDENT, INSTITUTE OF ADVANCED MEDIA ARTS AND SCIENCES
OGAKI, JAPAN

Hee Won Garden, Ho-Am Art Museum, Gyeonggi-do, Republic of Korea. JEAN CHUNG

# HONG KONG ZOOLOGICAL AND BOTANICAL GARDENS
## CENTRAL HONG KONG

FIRST OPENED TO THE PUBLIC IN 1864 THESE GROUNDS WERE FOUNDED AS A BOTANICAL GARDEN IN 1871 BEFORE BEING RENAMED IN 1975 AS A ZOOLOGICAL AND BOTANICAL GARDENS TO REFLECT THEIR INCREASING DEDICATION AND COMMITMENT TO ZOOLOGICAL STUDIES. COVERING MORE THAN 5.6 HECTARES, THESE BOTANICAL GARDENS INCLUDE A PLETHORA OF FLORA AND FAUNA INCLUDING A BAMBOO GROVE, CAMELLIA, MAGNOLIA AND AZALEA GARDENS, FOUNTAIN TERRACES, HERB GARDEN AND GREEN HOUSES, AND OF COURSE A HOST OF ANIMAL ENCLOSURES AND AN AVIARY. THE ZOOLOGICAL AND BOTANICAL COLLECTIONS IT HOUSES ARE COMPREHENSIVE AND FULLY DOCUMENTED AND ENSURE THAT ITS EDUCATIONAL PROGRAMMES ARE OF THE HIGHEST STANDARD PROVIDING AN ARENA FOR ACADEMICS AS WELL AS FOR SCHOOL CHILDREN.

Life in Hong Kong is so hectic, that everyone needs to find a place (or a few of them) where they can unwind. One such place for me is the Bing Tau Fa Yuen, or the "Garden of the General." This is what the Chinese residents of Hong Kong called the colony's first Botanic Garden, when it opened to the public in 1864. In 1975, it was renamed the Hong Kong Zoological and Botanical Gardens, to reflect its collection of rare mammals and reptiles, and is still Hong Kong's only zoo. Since I live nearby, I often take a brisk walk there early in the morning, or on Sundays, sit there in a more leisurely way with books or magazines, making this garden my own personal sanctuary.

Bing Tau Fa Yuen is a short walk downhill from my home although a steep, 62-metre climb for the office workers of Central. No matter how little or how much work it takes to get there, it is one of the loveliest outdoor places in urban Hong Kong, with a well-manicured and dense concentration of plant and bird species, as well as rare mammals and reptiles. Enterprising tourists, local runners, and parents watching over young children frequent its shady benches around a large fountain. Themed gardens cascade down the slope, featuring carefully labelled plantings of bamboo, magnolia, palms, orchids, azaleas, herbs and even a rare Dawn Redwood.

Small though it may be compared to its counterparts elsewhere in Asia and around the world, it is a serious working zoo. Useful work is done here on captive breeding and conservation of endangered species, and the animal residents are well-known friends to many in the neighbourhood. We think that "Siu Fa", the black jaguar, has not been happy since the passing of her partner "Siu Hak" in 2003, but the monkeys are as noisy and irreverent as ever. The most beautiful of the monkeys are clearly the Emperor, Golden Lion and Golden-Headed Tamarins, but the zoo's disdainful stars are its seven indolent-appearing Borneo orangutans, who slump disdainfully on their high ledges.

I always like to pay a visit to the exotic birds when I am in the garden. Where else could you see birds as emblematic of East and West as American Flamingoes and Red-crowned Cranes? The hot-pink flamingoes are like a Las Vegas song and dance act somehow gone astray. They posture, bow and bend their necks, run to and fro in a group and then suddenly take off on their own. I always wonder what they are up to.

The Red-crowned Crane, also called the Japanese or Manchurian crane, is the second-rarest bird in the world with a population of just 1,700-2,000. The mature bird is snow-white with a patch of skin on its cranium that turns bright red when it is angry or excited. The Japanese call this crane the *tancho* and emblazon it on the 100-yen note; you will see it also as the official logo of Japan Airlines. In China, the Red-crowned Crane is a symbol of longevity. Sages and immortals are often pictured riding on their wings. Reflecting this association, they are called *Xian He*, or "Fairy Cranes," and play an illustrious role in Chinese art and literature.

This garden is a daily renewal of "paradise found" for me...

**KAI-YIN LO**
JEWELLERY & ACCESSORIES DESIGNER, AUTHOR,
ART/CULTURE CONSULTANT
HONG KONG

# YU YUAN

ANREN JIE, SHANGHAI    PEOPLE'S REPUBLIC
OF CHINA

KNOWN AS "THE GARDEN OF CONTENTMENT", THIS 16TH CENTURY MING DYNASTY (1368-1644) GARDEN IS LOCATED IN THE CENTRE OF
SHANGHAI. IT WAS COMMISSIONED AND COMPLETED IN 1577 BY PAN YUNDUAN, A GOVERNMENT OFFICER, AS A PLACE FOR HIS PARENTS
TO RELAX. IT IS A PRIME EXAMPLE OF TRADITIONAL CHINESE LANDSCAPE DESIGN WITH NUMEROUS ROCKS, PONDS, TREE GARDENS AND
A MAZE OF DOORWAYS AND BRIDGES SEPARATING ONE GARDEN FROM THE NEXT. AFTER FALLING INTO DISREPAIR AT THE END OF THE
MING DYNASTY IT WAS BOUGHT BY RICH MERCHANTS IN 1760 WHO THEN SPENT MORE THAN 20 YEARS RESTORING THE GARDEN. IT WAS
FURTHER DESTROYED DURING THE OPIUM WARS OF THE 19TH CENTURY. WHAT WE SEE TODAY IS ABOUT HALF THE SIZE OF THE ORIGINAL
AND ALL MODERN RESTORATION WAS CONDUCTED OVER FIVE YEARS FROM 1956 AND HAS TRIED AS MUCH AS POSSIBLE TO STAY TRUE
TO ITS ORIGINAL FORM. IT WAS OPENED TO THE PUBLIC IN 1961.

Yu Garden is typical of the Jiangnan (south of the Yangtze River) classical gardens that are so famous in Suzhou. Nestled in the midst of high-rise buildings, lies this beautiful and delightful oasis of tranquility. That such an unusual, distinctly Chinese treasure still exists is particularly special in this bustling international city of commerce and trade. Shanghai is better known for its Bund and its Western architecture with emphasis on the city's European flavour.

Yu Garden was built almost 450 years ago by a senior official of a neighbouring province, a Mr. Pan, for his father to spend his remaining years. Pan began construction in 1559 and completed it in 1577 during the Ming Dynasty. By the time he finished the project, however, his father had died. Pan then retired there himself but had to sell the property soon thereafter as building and maintaining the garden impoverished him.

Yu Garden originally embraced almost 50,000 square metres with the Bridge of Nine Turnings located in the centre. This bridge is now located outside the present Yu Garden, which has been reduced through the centuries to only 20,000-plus square metres.

Within the present garden, there are only three remaining relics from the original garden.

The first is the large rock garden made of 2,000 tons of "Yellow Stone" from Zhejiang Province. The second is the Yu Ling Long rock in the centre facing Yu Hua Hall, the former study of Pan. It was said that Pan loved this rock so much that he chose to work or read in his study with his desk facing this rock so that he could enjoy it whenever he looked up. The third is the ginkgo biloba tree in front of Wanhua Chamber which is located in one of the courtyards.

Many of the buildings and trees date back to the Qing Dynasty three hundred years ago. Although the remaining beautiful landscapes, ponds and buildings cannot claim the same antiquity, the garden nevertheless was lovingly reconstructed and still retains its ancient flavour.

**NORA SUN**
PRESIDENT, NORA SUN ASSOCIATES LTD.
SHANGHAI, PEOPLE'S REPUBLIC OF CHINA

# LIU YUAN

SUZHOU, JIANGSU PEOPLE'S REPUBLIC OF CHINA

"THE LINGERING GARDEN" OR LIU YUAN WAS BUILT DURING THE MING DYNASTY (1368-1644) IN THE 16TH CENTURY. IT IS THE LARGEST AND MOST IMPORTANT CLASSICAL GARDEN IN SUZHOU AND ONE OF THE FOUR MOST FAMOUS GARDENS IN CHINA. IT WAS ORIGINALLY BUILT BY A RETIRED OFFICIAL CALLED XU TAI WHO INCORPORATED MANY ODDLY SHAPED ROCKS IN THE GARDEN, ONE OF WHICH IS MORE THAN 20 FT TALL. DURING THE QING DYNASTY (1644-1911) IT WAS BOUGHT BY LIU SHU WHO HAD MASTERPIECES CARVED INTO BOTH SIDES OF THE CORRIDORS. SUCCESSIVE OWNERS HAVE ADDED THEIR OWN INTERPRETATION TO THE GARDEN BUT MAINTAINED AND FOLLOWED THE EXISTING ARCHITECTURE AND LAYOUT. THE GOVERNMENT HAS OVERSEEN THE RESTORATION WORK ON THE GARDEN WE SEE NOW AND LIU YUAN WAS DECLARED A WORLD HERITAGE SITE BY UNESCO IN 1997.

"Artful, because it borrows from and blends in with existing surroundings; exquisite, because it accentuates the uniqueness and beauties of the chosen locale"—a saying coined during the Ming Dynasty, aptly points out the defining essence of China's classic gardens, especially the delicate beauty of Liu Yuan—the Lingering Garden in Suzhou. The beauty of Liu Yuan is found not in any grandness of scale or atmosphere, but rather in the ethereal sense of finding "vast expanses within a narrow space" and "a panorama of scenic nature all within a stone's throw."

First built during the Ming Dynasty, Liu Yuan has survived many wars and undergone numerous renovations, and remains today one of the most artfully crafted private traditional Chinese gardens. Located in the middle of a bustling city, this soulful place that was once a private residence reflects the scholar-bureaucrat's yearning for "a taste of nature without leaving the city." The spatial arrangements of the various scenes in the garden are so ingeniously designed that, as one promenades along its 700-metre winding verandah, the seamless transitions from one scene to the next will plunge the visitor into continuous discoveries of brave new worlds at almost every bend of the path.

The warm and moist local climate has blessed the landscape with thriving lushness, to which the ancient architects had wisely adapted the overall structure of the various buildings in the garden, such that the natural and the man-made are harmonised in a most pleasing symphony of visual beauty. Permeating every fibre of the place is a sense of perfection: that everything is in its place; that there exists an imperturbable harmony between its movement and stillness; that there is deliberate artistic endeavour behind everything that seems so casually and randomly placed. You will find the traditional Chinese painting coming to life in "The Twelve Peaks of Taihu" *(Taihushi Shier Feng)*, built from rocks native to the Taihu Lake, while "The Peony Dais" *(Mudan Huatai)*, built in the Ming Dynasty, is a sight not to be missed in spring, when the whole dais is aflame with peony blossoms in full bloom and dancing to the ageless tune of the spring breeze to evoke in the beholder a reminiscent yearning for the beauty of ages past. Other must-see sights in Liu Yuan include "Little Paradise" *(Xiao Penglai*, or *Little Penglai Island)*, *Zizai Chu* (literally, 'a place to be at ease'), and Ke Ting Pavillion *(Ke Ting)*."

"Though by human hands it came to be, yet a fruit of nature it appears"—every little inch of the beautiful Liu Yuan is a manifestation of the boundless art of the traditional Chinese garden.

**PROFESSOR PAN, GONG-KAI**
PRESIDENT, CENTRAL ACADEMY OF FINE ARTS
BEIJING, PEOPLE'S REPUBLIC OF CHINA

# JI CHANG YUAN

WUXI, JIANGSU PEOPLE'S REPUBLIC OF CHINA

SET IN XIHUI PARK, JI CHANG YUAN, "THE GARDEN OF ECSTASY" OR "GARDEN FOR EASE OF MIND," WAS BUILT BY THE QIN FAMILY IN THE 16TH CENTURY AND MAKES SPECTACULAR USE OF TWO HILLS AND THE EASTERN LAKE. IT WAS RENOVATED AT THE BEGINNING OF THE QING DYNASTY (1644-1911) AND A SERIES OF ARTIFICIAL HILLS WAS CREATED BY MOUNTAIN DESIGNER ZHANG LIAN AND HIS NEPHEW. THE SHEER SIZE OF THE GARDEN AND THE MAGNIFICATION OF THIS THROUGH THE NATURAL GEOGRAPHY OF THE AREA ATTRACTED MANY EMPERORS AND IN 1751 THE QIANLONG EMPEROR COMMISSIONED A REPLICA OF IT. JIA SHU TANG—HALL OF BEAUTIFUL TREES, AND THE TEA HOUSE ARE CONSIDERED TWO OF THE BEST GARDENS WITHIN THIS VAST GARDEN.

Breezes in spring,
Flowers in summer,
Moon in autumn,
Snow in winter

One of the very first things I did when I took over the site for the China Club in Peking was to plant blossoms in the courtyards, which were effectively the inner gardens of this modest princely palace from the early Qing Dynasty. It was particularly important that the blossom trees stand prominently in the first courtyard, as nothing beats the overwhelming and immediate welcome of flowering blossoms in the spring—with a wondrously delicate scent in the air; with petals from the blossoms and dancing pollen from the stalks drifting across the gentlest breeze, with eyes feasting on an abundance of colours in red and white. These pleasures encapsulate for me a quintessence of a Chinese garden, in tranquility and serenity, not to mention symbolism. For us Chinese have always loved symbolism and whenever artists painted, they invariably juxtaposed the images with poetry. Shitao was a master with peach blossoms and in one of his scrolls, he wrote:-

*Spring breeze and gentle rain come to the window of my mountain lodge;*
*Even now, I paint peach blossoms in their colourful attire.*
*I laugh at myself that in spite of old age I have not learned to live with leisure,*
*And must still play with my brush to pass the time.*

Mind you, sometimes artists were a little more melancholic, even with blossoms. Qian Xuan, a Chinese painter in the 13th century, had painted a pear blossom to symbolise an ageing woman crying in the rain. She had been a beautiful courtesan, but was now merely surviving under the nadir of the Song Dynasty and the impending Mongol invasion. But it was a poignant image and one which a Chinese garden somehow always manages to evoke.

So, in order to remind myself and others of the yin and yang of life, we now have both a peach blossom and a pear blossom in our first courtyard garden of the China Club. Whenever they blossom, I always make a special pilgrimage to see them in their subtle and sublime beauty.

**SIR DAVID TANG**
ENTREPRENEUR & FOUNDER, CHINA CLUB, SHANGHAI TANG
HONG KONG

# IMPERIAL GARDENS, JING SHAN GONG YUAN INCLUDING BEI HAI PARK

BEIJING PEOPLE'S REPUBLIC OF CHINA

THIS IMPERIAL GARDEN, KNOWN BY MANY NAMES INCLUDING "PROSPECT HILL", "FENG SHUI PARK" AND "COAL HILL PARK" (THE LATTER A DIRECT CHINESE TRANSLATION), WAS ORIGINALLY PART OF THE FORBIDDEN CITY AND DATES FROM THE LATE 12TH CENTURY. THE DOMINATING HILL IN THE CENTRE OF THE PARK WAS CREATED IN 1420 WHEN THE EMPEROR HEARD THAT A HILL POSITIONED BEHIND THE FORBIDDEN CITY WOULD IMPROVE ITS FENG SHUI. THE SOIL FOR THE HILL, KNOWN AS THE MOUNTAIN OF A MYRIAD LIFE, IS ALL FROM THE EXCAVATION FOR THE MOAT AROUND THE IMPERIAL PALACE AND NEARBY CANALS. IN 1644 THE LAST MING EMPEROR HUNG HIMSELF FROM A TREE ON THIS HILL; THE FOLLOWING QING DYNASTY (1644-1912) RENAMED THE HILL JING SHAN, THE MOUNTAIN OF PERSPECTIVE. UNTIL THE EARLY PART OF THE 20TH CENTURY, THE PARK LAY DIRECTLY NEXT TO THE MOAT AND THE FORBIDDEN CITY. HOWEVER, ROAD BUILDING IN 1928 PERMANENTLY SEPARATED THE PARK FROM THE FORBIDDEN CITY.

The essence of Chinese gardening is the harmony between natural and artificial beauty. Landscape, architecture, greenery, and literature (including painting and calligraphy) are the indispensable four elements of a traditional Chinese garden. Unlike the delicate private gardens in Southern China, the Imperial gardens in Beijing are of an extensive magnitude and evoke a grand presence. This is even true in the names of the lakes and temples as the emperors named them after legendary places in heaven, believing that they had been sent from there to rule the Central Kingdom.

The gardens were meant to be poetic from different perspectives and at different times or during different seasons; in addition to this, poems were written to give titles to the buildings as well as the different scenery depicted.

The mountains in these gardens are mostly made of the mud dug from the lakes. At the highest point of the mountain, there is usually a dominant piece of architecture denoting the geographical and spiritual centre; these include the White Pagoda at Bei Hai Park and Buddha Fragrance Temple at the Summer Palace. Water, which accounts for half or even more of the space in the gardens, has been beautified by bridges, small islands, and fully-decorated covered corridors around it. In the more private parts of the gardens that originally were exclusively used by the Imperial ladies, there are small water-lily ponds decorated by unusually shaped Tai-Hu Lake Stones. In the theatres, tea and snacks were served and Peking-Opera was performed to amuse the Royal family.

For five dynasties dating back to roughly one thousand years ago, Chinese emperors built and rebuilt these parks in the capital city. They dedicated some pavilions to their mothers, or Buddhist towers to mark the visits of religious leaders. The last emperor of the Ming Dynasty  hanged himself from a tree at Jing Shan Park, because he couldn't bear the view of the rebels taking over the Forbidden City only a few hundred yards away. Some of the parks, like Yuan Ming Yuan, are sadly in ruins and few relics survive,  as they were burnt down by foreign invading forces.

**YANG, LAN**
CHAIRPERSON, SUN MEDIA GROUP & SUN CULTURAL FOUNDATION
BEIJING, PEOPLE'S REPUBLIC OF CHINA

# SOSWAEWON GARDEN

DAMYANG-GUN, JEOLLANAM-DO  REPUBLIC OF KOREA

SOSWAEWON WAS CREATED BY THE SCHOLAR YANG SAN-BO IN THE 14TH CENTURY DURING THE JOSEON PERIOD (1392-1910). IT TOOK 70 YEARS TO COMPLETE AND IS HIGHLY REPRESENTATIVE OF GARDENS BUILT DURING THIS PERIOD, MAKING EXTENSIVE USE OF NATURAL FEATURES. COVERING 9,900-SQUARE-METRES, THE GARDEN COMPRISES THICK BAMBOO GROVES, WOODS, FLOWER BEDS AND PONDS. IT IS SURROUNDED BY NATURAL BOULDERS, AND WITHIN THE PARK YOU CAN FIND THE GWANGPUNGGAK PAVILION, JEWOLDANG HALL, AS WELL AS A SINGLE-LOG BRIDGE AND A WATER WHEEL.

Soswaewon Garden was built during the reign of King Jungjong (reign 1506-1544) of the Joseon Dynasty by the Confucian scholar Yang, San-bo (1503-1557). After the death of his mentor Jo, Gwang-jo (1482-1519), Yang renounced all further worldly ambitions and spent his days in exile at Soswaewon. Like other gardens of the period, Soswaewon reflects a naturalistic approach to garden design. By incorporating many natural elements in their "original" state, Yang created an "idyllic" place where visitors would feel immersed in nature's beauty and harmony. At the same time, Soswaewon also served as a meeting ground where disillusioned scholars could exchange ideas during a period of political turmoil.

The Korean words *Soswae* mean "clean and cool". A small waterfall, which flows through the centre of the garden, is flanked by two pavilions, Gwangpunggak Pavilion and Jewoldang Hall, which are built on the surrounding slopes. A dense bamboo grove lines the path approaching the garden. The garden design features the Yeonji Pond and the Jeongcheon Stream. An aqueduct made from bamboo spans the ford. There are also simple constructed elements such as a single-log bridge, a watermill and Daebongdae, the thatch roof pavilion. The garden woods consist of aged pine, zelkova, maple and peach trees. The walls enclosing the garden are made of stone and mud and are engraved with poetry and calligraphy.

Banana plants, camellias, paulownias, ginkgoes, willows, and lotuses transform the scenery throughout the year, highlighting variations in the natural foliage during different seasons. Included in the garden flora are the "Four Gracious Plants", plum, orchid, chrysanthemum and bamboo, representing the honour of the *seonbi* of the Joseon period. The gentleman scholar aspired to lead an austere, stoic and solitary life, dedicated to seeking harmony with nature and upholding social traditions. The garden reflects the values of its former inhabitants; there are no artificial accoutrements. With its extensive incorporation of the natural elements found in its surrounding environment, Soswaewon is a timeless garden, whose appearance today is probably not much different from what it was almost half a millennium earlier.

**CHUNG, MYUNG-WHUN**
PRINCIPAL CONDUCTOR, SEOUL PHILHARMONIC ORCHESTRA
SEOUL, REPUBLIC OF KOREA

# CHOLLIPO ARBORETUM

SOSAN GUN, CHUNGCHEONGNAM-DO REPUBLIC OF KOREA

STARTED IN 1970 CHOLLIPO ARBORETUM HAS BECOME THE LIFE WORK OF MIN PYONG GAL, FORMERLY AN AMERICAN KNOWN AS CARL FERRIS MILLER. STARTING WITH INSTALLING AND RESTORING SOME KOREAN TRADITIONAL BUILDINGS HE WISHED TO PRESERVE FOR HERITAGE, MIN WENT ON TO PLANT TREES AND SHRUBS ON THIS BARREN, SANDY STRETCH. WITH THE ACQUISITION OF MORE SURROUNDING LAND, THE ARBORETUM STARTED TAKING SHAPE AFTER 1973. COVERING SOME 60 HECTARES, IT NOW INCLUDES FORESTED MOUNTAINS, CULTIVATED FARM FIELDS AND RICE PADDIES, SAND-DUNES AND A 5 HECTARE ISLAND WHICH IS ACCESSIBLE BY FOOT DURING LOW TIDE. IT ALSO HAS ONE OF THE FINEST COLLECTION OF MAGNOLIAS IN THE WORLD (MORE THAN 1,800).

"From so simple a beginning," wrote Charles Darwin in the last sentence of *The Origin of Species.* The origin of Chollipo Arboretum was simple indeed. In 1962 an American expatriate and born-again Korean Pyong-gal Min (formerly Carl Ferris Miller) bought 5 acres of land in a small fishing village called Chollipo, with plans to build a cottage there someday. Little did he know that one of the most beautiful and valuable botanical gardens in the world would evolve from so simple a beginning.

Chollipo Arboretum is a living Ark created by a modern-day Santa Claus. Mr. Min was born on 24 December 1921, and his creation represents an extraordinary gift to the Korean people and the environment. The Arboretum now sprawls over 60 hectares of sand dunes, rice paddies, cultivated farmlands, forested mountains, and a 5-hectare island, harbouring a good mixture of indigenous and exotic woody and herbaceous plants. The climate is mild with temperatures rarely dropping below -10°C, which distinguishes the area from most temperate regions in the eastern United States and Europe. The Arboretum is soaked by monsoon rains every summer and baked by the sun through long dry autumns. It is a near-ideal place to anchor an Ark for a diversity of temperate plants.

Chollipo Arboretum is particularly famous for its collections of magnolias and hollies. The internationally renowned magnolia collection is the world's most comprehensive, with up to 450 species, hybrids and named cultivars. Visitors believing that magnolias are just precocious plants flowering in early spring will be amazed by the year-round feast of magnolia colours at Chollipo. The Arboretum also contains more than 90% of all known species of hollies. In recent years the Arboretum's name has frequently been on the lips of horticulturists, because its creation, an evergreen euonymus commonly called "Chollipo", is becoming a popular household plant.

Chollipo Arboretum was created by a man, but its plants are left untouched by human hands according to the creator's strict orders. Mr. Min respected the traditional Korean style of gardening, which involves adapting to the ways of trees. "Trees are trees," he used to say. When you visit Chollipo Arboretum, be prepared to become a part of Nature, not its ruler.

**PROFESSOR CHOE, JAE CHUN**
UNIVERSITY CHAIR PROFESSOR, EWHA WOMAN'S UNIVERSITY
SEOUL, REPUBLIC OF KOREA

# HEE WON GARDEN AT HO-AM ART MUSEUM

YONGIN-SI, GYEONGGI-DO REPUBLIC OF KOREA

IN 1982 THE HO-AM ART MUSEUM WAS ESTABLISHED BY THE LATE LEE BYUNG, THE FOUNDER OF THE SAMSUNG GROUP, AS THE COUNTRY'S FIRST PRIVATE ART MUSEUM. IN 1997 THE GARDEN OF HEE WON WAS CULTIVATED AROUND THE MUSEUM AND TODAY IS REGARDED AS ONE OF THE FINEST EXAMPLES OF KOREAN TRADITIONAL GARDEN DESIGN. THE "STONE IMAGE PATH," WHICH GUIDES VISITORS TO THE ENTRANCE OF THE HO-AM ART MUSEUM, IS MOST BEAUTIFUL IN SPRING AND AUTUMN AND INCLUDES LARGE WORKS BY BOURDELLE. HEE WON ITSELF IS BEAUTIFUL AND ELEGANT AND COMPRISES OF ESSENTIAL ELEMENTS OF TRADITIONAL ARCHITECTURE, SUCH AS A STONE PLATFORM, A PAVILION, A POND AND A WALL. A VARIETY OF TREES AND WILD FLOWERS CAN BE SEEN AND IN JUNE MAGNIFICENT LOTUS FLOWERS BLOOM IN THE POND IN FRONT OF THE MUSEUM.

It is difficult to reduce the characteristics of Korean gardens to a simple summary as Korean gardens are inseparably tied to the local site. At Hee Won Garden, the landscape, once altered into ordinary lawn, was to be transformed radically by adding depth, and blending the grand museum building into the foot of the mountain. With respect to the theory of "borrowed landscape" which formed the basis of Korean traditional landscape design, the Hee Won was built with its original contours restored.

The Hee Won is composed of three zones: the first zone is the main garden area with sequences of specific gardens and transition areas which present details and production principles, the second is composed of a close-up view of the main garden area and panoramic distant views, with a lakeside garden beyond the wall; also including a garden path, a stand, and a picnic area arranged between the garden wall and the lake. The third one reveals surrounding mountains and a transplanted pine forest. While wandering through the main garden area, viewers can appreciate the lush variety of landscape views. Visitors start their journey at the main gate in the western side of the Hee Won, entering into a transition area, a bamboo grove and white garden, then arrive in a small garden, main garden, and the museum area, step by step. Wanderers on the high stone platform can choose to return or continue their journey along the valley of a stream which flows east to the forest.

The southern lake, joined to mountains as if they were lips, contain a shadow of the mountains. A brook winds and stretches to the west and disappears through a willow grove. Undulating mountains wait in the distance. These may be the most sublime landscape elements the Hee Won possesses. For that scenic beauty to be ushered in as much as possible, the walls, steps and observatories, like stone platforms and arbours by the water, were manipulated and adjusted to allow visitors to appreciate it from a variety of vantage points.

The wall in Korean garden architecture functions as a frame of landscape. In spring, the surface of the lake is full of cherry and apricot blossoms; in fall, the foliage is intoxicating; in winter, flocks of ducks gather between the water and the mountains. People along the lakeside or in the front yard of the art gallery, or even at the teahouse, enjoy the view in all seasons.

A long road beside the lake winds through cherry blossoms. A platform of stacked stones by the water awaits a couple of pavilions that will be built. Twisting many times from the west, the road to the front yard of the museum arrives outside the rear garden. Gates, stairs, walls and pavilions alternate. In other words, despite the narrow space between the lake, mountains and the museum, artificially wrinkled terrain features in the garden complex allow viewers to appreciate various aspects of the landscape. Like wandering poets in the thick mist, people are often mesmerised by the beauty of the mystic composition of the garden.

While the landscape design draws the natural scenery into the garden, and sets trees around the buildings, the architecture intends not to reveal its existence from the entrance. To achieve this gradual appearance of the roofs, ridges and eaves beyond, not only are there various architectural elements such as layered walls framing the existing forest, a retaining wall for the main building of the museum layered like stone stairs with wild flowers on every step and a six-metre stone platform, but also a transformation of the topography was necessary. The man-made mounds were based on the original terrain before the museum had been built, but the height of them was designed in accordance with the perspective distance from the museum building. The mounds, in other words, a new main structure of the garden and a metaphor of the yang element in the site, are aimed to encompass all visual experiences. Predictably, the position of the original gate was changed. The stone platform, which replaced the central part of the lawn to consist of stony stairs on the inclined road, added a more mystic atmosphere around the existing museum building by partly screening it from the visitors. Water, the blood of the garden and the source of energy, issues from mountains behind to embrace all the gardens with its yin liveliness. Just like the blood circulation of a human body, water flows high and low through the Stream Valley and gathers at the ponds of the garden.

The aboriginal pine trees and willows were transplanted from the mountain behind to the garden to rehabilitate the original terrain features of mountains. Native plants and flowers add more wildness and naturalness to the garden. Four gracious plants symbolise the virtue of scholars; green plum trees, orchids, chrysanthemums and bamboo were planted along the periphery of the six-metre stone platform. The stone figures, such as images of Buddhism, pagodas, temple lanterns and folk articles with motifs of folk stories, sit shyly in cozy corners of the Hee Won. The predominant material of the stone figure collection is granite which has been abundant in Korea for centuries. The Hee Won is not just a garden full of native plants but also an open museum displaying Korean stone figures harmonising with Korean landscape tastefully. The granite figures, just like the other architectural elements in the garden, repeatedly hide and reveal themselves on the trails in the reclusive scenery of the Hee Won.

**PROFESSOR JUNG, YOUNG-SUN**
PRESIDENT OF STL (SEOAHN TOTAL LANDSCAPE)
SEOUL, REPUBLIC OF KOREA

# CHANGDEOKGUNG (CHANGDEOK PALACE)

SEOUL REPUBLIC OF KOREA

THE "PALACE OF PROSPERING VIRTUE" WAS FIRST BUILT IN THE 15TH CENTURY AND WAS REBUILT IN 17TH CENTURY AFTER THE OLD PALACE WAS BURNT DOWN BY THE JAPANESE. IT IS ONE OF FIVE GRAND PALACES USED BY THE KINGS OF THE JOSEON DYNASTY (1392-1910) AND WAS ORIGINALLY A DETACHED PALACE WITHIN THE GROUNDS BUILT FOR THE CROWN PRINCE. THE BIWON OR "SECRET GARDEN", ADJACENT TO THE PALACE, WAS BUILT DURING THE YI DYNASTY FOR USE EXCLUSIVELY BY THE ROYAL FAMILY AND THE KINGS' CONCUBINES. THIS MAGICAL AREA OF WINDING PATHS LINKING THE WOODED SLOPES WITH LOTUS PONDS AND PAVILIONS IS TRULY ONE OF THE BEST EXAMPLES OF TRADITIONAL KOREAN NATURAL LANDSCAPE DESIGNS. IT IS FAMOUS FOR ITS CENTURIES OLD TREES, INCLUDING ONE MORE THAN 1000 YEARS OLD AND A 700-YEAR-OLD JUNIPER TREE. CHANGDEOKGUNG WAS LISTED BY UNESCO IN 1997 AS A WORLD CULTURAL HERITAGE SITE.

Biwon, or the Secret Garden, in Changdeok Palace, is an "oasis" located in the heart of downtown Seoul, a city of twelve million people and the capital city of the Republic of Korea.

Seoul had also been the capital of the Joseon Dynasty (1392-1910) when several palaces were built for its Kings and royal family members. Changdeok Palace is one of the major palaces built soon after the establishment of the dynasty in 1392. Its construction was begun in 1406, but many of its buildings and pavilions had been added through the centuries that followed. The extension of the boundaries of the palace was completed by the early 17th century.

Biwon is also known as the "Forbidden Garden" *(Keumwon)* as the entrance to it was strictly forbidden to people other than the immediate family members of the reigning king. Its wooded areas, paths, pavilions and ponds are exquisite and stately at the same time.

Today, the garden is open to the public and is entered through the grounds of the Changdeok Palace along the wall which separates the palace from the adjoining Changgeyong Palace. The wall, made of stones and topped with gray earthenware tiled roofs, is one of the most beautiful features of traditional Korean architecture. It was made to follow the ups and downs of the terrain with differing heights. As one enters into the Garden, one forgets the fact that he or she is in the capital of a bustling 21st-century city. Its pristine ground of pounded light earth, trees hundreds of years old, large and small pavilions by the pond which produces a clear mirror-like reflection, large boulders by the creeks and fountains, buildings clad with traditional *dancheong* colouring or just plain wooden colours, are just a few of the Garden's exceptionally beautiful features.

Perhaps the best known section of the garden is where two contrasting structures stand on either side of the Buyong-ji pond: Buyong-jeong pavilion and the two-story Juhap-ru pavilion. The Buyong-jeong, or the pavilion of Rose of Sharon, is smaller and the more exquisite of the two. Originally, it was built in 1707, during the reign of King Sukjong (reign 1674-1720), but was rebuilt in 1792 during the reign of King Jeongjo (reign 1776-1800). Buyong-jeong has a plan resembling a Greek cross, and the two columns that support the pavilion rise from the square-shaped Buyong-ji pond in front of it. In the middle of the pond, there is a circular island with a pine tree which adds to the beauty of the pond and the pavilion. The reflection of the roofs of the pavilion on the pond is so clear it is as if we are looking at an upside-down photo.

In East Asian cosmology, the square represents the earth while the circle symbolises heaven, so the large two-storey building across the pond was named Juhap-ru, or the Pavilion of Harmony with the Universe. The suffix *ru* means a high multi-storied structure. It is the largest structure in the garden, built in 1777 during the reign of King Jeongjo who at some point used the building to house part of the royal library.

As we walk toward the north from this area to the heart of the Garden, we come to another pond. Shaped approximately like the Korean Peninsula, it has the name Bando-ji, or the "Peninsula Pond." On one side of its "shore," there is a pavilion which has a fan-shaped plan, the only pavilion of its kind in Korea. Two of its columns rise from the pond as is the case with Buyong-jeong. The name of the pavilion is Gwanram-jeong, or the Pavilion where one moors one's boat and watches the scenery around. The suffix *jeong* means pavilion, but it has the same pronunciation as another character meaning to stop or rest. Therefore, in a large garden such as this, one strolls around for a while or rides a boat on a pond and rests at the pavilion when tired.

The last structure introduced here is an unusual element in a garden. Gyeongyeon-dang house is a residence of 99 *kan*, *kan* being a unit of measure for space approximately 9 square metres. During the Joseon Dynasty, there was an injunction against building a house over 100 *kan* among the general population as such a large house would compete with royal palaces. Gyeongyeon-dang was built in 1828 during the reign of King Sunjo (reign 1800-1834) as the king wished to taste the life of non-royal folks from time to time. So the house has no *dancheong* colouring on its wooden parts as ordinary homes were prohibited to have luxurious colouring. Its small-sized rooms and subdued natural wooden colours put the house in a class of its own amongst other buildings within the Garden.

Biwon, being a garden within a royal palace, is exceptionally large compared to other traditional gardens of Korea, but everything in it is at human scale compared to Chinese royal gardens. Also, it is much more natural in the creation of details compared to Japanese gardens. It is a sophisticated man-made garden, but it maintains aspects of nature at its best.

**PROFESSOR DR. YI, SONG-MI**
PROFESSOR EMERITA OF ART HISTORY, THE ACADEMY OF KOREAN STUDIES
SEOUL, REPUBLIC OF KOREA

# BYODO-IN

UJI CITY, KYOTO JAPAN

BYODO-IN WAS ORIGINALLY BUILT IN 998 AS A RURAL VILLA FOR ONE OF THE MOST POWERFUL MEMBERS OF THE FUJIWARA CLAN, THE VILLA WAS CONVERTED INTO A BUDDHIST TEMPLE IN THE 11TH CENTURY. LISTED ON THE UNESCO WORLD HERITAGE LIST IN 1994, BYODO-IN IS A "PURE LAND" GARDEN, JYODO STYLE, A TYPE OF GARDEN POPULAR DURING THE HEIAN PERIOD (794-1192) AND ONE OF THE FEW REMAINING JAPANESE PURE LAND FORM GARDENS TODAY. THE MAIN BUILDING, THE AMIDA HALL OR PHOENIX HALL WAS BUILT IN 1053 AND IS CONSIDERED A NATIONAL TREASURE. IT IS THE ONLY BUILDING IN THE GROUNDS DATING FROM THIS PERIOD AS MOST OF THE OTHER STRUCTURES OF THE PERIOD WERE BURNT DOWN DURING A CIVIL WAR IN THE 14TH CENTURY. THE MONASTERY GARDEN AND THE AJIIKE POND IN FRONT OF THE PHOENIX HALL WERE DESIGNED TO RECREATE PARADISE ON EARTH, AND THE LANDSCAPE USED AS A MODEL INCLUDE THE UJI RIVER AND THE HILLS BEYOND IT.

This garden tells me that ancient generosity relates to modern transparency, or that the early affection for nature has much in common with modern-day minimalism.

The aim of the creator of this garden was to bring a paradise on earth. This is not an uncommon theme. The approach of utilising water to bring a paradise into view is also not rare; Hadrian's Villa in Rome is one of the renowned gardens designed to create a paradise on earth with the use of water.

I like the Byodo-In Temple garden because of its lightness, which is projected by the floating building. By contrast, Hadrian's Villa attained geometric order by using a stone called travertine, but it could not achieve the lightness apparent in the Byodo-In Temple, a lightness which stems from the use of wood as a material.

European gardens, like those of Hadrian's Villa, only attained a similar lightness much later—during the 20th century when they began to move out of stone as a building material towards the greater flexibility that iron allowed.

It is interesting to see the role that Byodo-In Temple has played in the evolution of the concept of lightness in European gardens. In 1893, the Columbus Expo was held in Chicago. In this Expo, Japanese carpenters built the wooden Japanese Pavilion modeled after Byodo-In Ho-O-Do in the solemn atmosphere of a venue themed on pure white Roman-style buildings. The contrast in design between the Japanese Pavilion and other buildings at once drew everybody's attention. The Japanese Pavilion also featured a pond after the original Byodo-In Temple.

One American had a life-changing experience when he visited the Japan Pavilion. His name was Frank Lloyd Wright, a leading American architect counted among the pioneers of modernist buildings in the 20th century. His work prior to the Japan Pavilion experience followed the typical American colonial style.

After viewing the Japan Pavilion he got rid of the heavy box-like structures and made a drastic shift to the light "Byodo-In" style. This change did not remain confined to Wright alone; the expansive style he created had a considerable impact on European architects in general. People say the Barcelona Pavilion designed by Mies van der Rohe could not have emerged without the influence of Wright.

The Barcelona Pavilion is a paradise on earth with a structure as slim and delicate as a wooden building, and is also accompanied by a pond. What is more interesting is that the stone used for the floor around the pond of the Barcelona Pavilion is also the same travertine used for Hadrian's Villa. And so, through these transitions introduced by two geniuses, Wright and Mies, both Hadrian's Villa and the Byodo-In Temple have finally completed a circular ring. The basic structure of the Old Imperial Hotel, Tokyo designed by Wright much later (1922) is very similar to the one at Byodo-In Ho-O-Do. All this shows that gardens and buildings also make repeated transmigrations.

**KENGO KUMA**
ARCHITECT AND FOUNDER, KENGO KUMA & ASSOCIATES
TOKYO, JAPAN

# KINKAKU-JI
## KYOTO JAPAN

KINKAKU-JI OR "THE TEMPLE OF THE GOLDEN PAVILION" IS THE POPULAR NAME OF ROKUON-JI (DEER PARK TEMPLE), A TEMPLE DEDICATED TO THE BUDDHIST GODDESS OF MERCY. IN 1994 IT WAS LISTED BY UNESCO ON THEIR WORLD HERITAGE LIST. BUILT IN 1397 AS A RETIREMENT VILLA FOR SHOGUN ASHIKAGA YOSHIMITSU, THE VILLA WAS CONVERTED INTO A ZEN TEMPLE OF THE RINZAI SCHOOL BY HIS SON. KINKAKU-JI FEATURES A THREE-STORY PAVILION COVERED IN GOLD LEAF WITH A ROOF TOPPED BY A PHOENIX, BUILT ON THE EDGE OF A KYOKOCHI OR MIRROR POND. THIS BUILDING ACTUALLY DATES FROM 1955 AS A FANATICAL MONK BURNT DOWN THE FORMER TEMPLE IN 1950. HOWEVER, THE GARDENS AND LAKE, DESIGNED TO REFLECT SCENES OF BUDDHIST PARADISE, STAY VERY MUCH TRUE TO THEIR ORIGINAL FORM. MOVING THROUGH THESE GARDENS, OTHER TEMPLES, SHRINES AND PAGODAS BECOME VISIBLE, BLENDING MAGICALLY WITH THE HARMONY OF NATURE.

The Kinkaku-ji Temple garden is one with a pond, which we can walk around. During our stroll, we can enjoy, as a centre-piece, the Rokuon-ji-Shariden (Kinkaku or Golden Pavilion), covered in gold leaf, and its reflection on the Kyokochi Pond which surrounds the Kinkaku, together with Mount Kinugasa which rises beyond the Kinkaku as a scenic backdrop to the garden. The Kinkaku-ji Temple garden is counted as one of the masterpieces of the strolling pond garden—but it might be more than just that.

When viewing the garden from the first floor of the Kinkaku, which is called *Hosuiin* in Shinden-Zukuri style, the whole panorama of the Kyokochi Pond framed by pillars and *Shitomi-do* (latticed wooden shutters) sweeps into view. The beauty of this spectacle is a feature of the garden style, which should be gazed at in a sitting position. This is why the Kinkaku-ji Temple garden might not be merely a strolling pond garden. The panoramic views consist of stones of various sizes in the pond including a miniature island called Ashiwarajima, with maple and pine trees depicting the four seasons, in the background.

From *Hosuiin*, the first floor of the Kinkaku, this pond garden can be enjoyed at a level close to the surface of the pond. It is said that the nobles of the day used to enjoy poems and musical performances from boats on the pond when the Kinkaku was just built. As such, the eye line from the current *Hosuiin* might be quite close to the view these nobles had in their time.

Once we step in the Kinkaku and view the pond garden, the Kinkaku itself goes out of focus and scenery beyond our ordinary sense of scale emerges due to the low eye level. This scenery is very colourful and lively although Kinkaku is not within view. It can be said that this scenery is a "symbolic miniature landscape garden" unique to the Rokuon-ji garden, unlike the "mystical landscaped gardens" of China and the "naturalistic landscaped gardens" of England.

The feature of the symbolic miniature landscape method is to embody nature symbolically instead of depicting nature as itself. The abstracting/deformation methodology—creating an ideal imaginary landscape by deforming and encoding the real landscape—can be seen in every aspect of Japanese culture and art. It can be said that the layout of ingredients in a Japanese bowl and the framing layout or emphasis lines used in Japanese comics are also highly abstracted.

When looking at the Kinkaku-ji Temple garden from such a perspective, we can see that this garden incorporates many elements in a multi-layered way and is totally distinct from abstract art, as typified by the Karesansui garden, which encodes elements into graphical artwork.

Looking back toward the Kinkaku, different architectural styles, namely, Shinden-Zukuri for the 1st floor, Shoin-Zukuri for the 2nd floor and the Karayo Style for the 3rd floor, are collaged onto one building. This collage art seems to have achieved an abstract effect as a result of being covered with gold leaf, which disorientates the viewer's visual sense.

This abstraction causes a mental overload on the viewer to the point of slipping into a trance-like state through the profusion of diverse images, akin to the psychedelic designs of the 60's.

The garden, the Kinkaku, and the pond on which the Kinkaku is reflected—we are dazzled by a super-abundance of visual information, just like watching the scene of the Star Gate in *2001: A Space Odyssey*.

Let's allow ourselves to re-interpret the concept of a traditional garden from the perspective of modern people—that may be the fun of viewing the garden.

**NAOKI TERADA**
ARCHITECT AND FOUNDER, TERADA DESIGN
TOKYO, JAPAN

# SAIHO-JI

KYOTO JAPAN

DESCRIBED AS THE OLDEST SURVIVING EXAMPLE OF A 12TH CENTURY PARADISE GARDEN, AND THE OLDEST MOST IMPORTANT GARDEN OF THE MUROMACHI PERIOD (1336-1573), SAIHO-JI IS ALSO KNOWN AS KOKE-DERE OR "THE MOSS GARDEN" AND WAS ORIGINALLY FOUNDED IN THE 8TH CENTURY. IT WAS LATER REFURBISHED IN THE 14TH CENTURY BY A MONK AND ZEN LANDSCAPE GARDENER, MUSO KOKUSHI/SOSEKI, AS A STROLL GARDEN. LISTED ON THE UNESCO WORLD HERITAGE LIST IN 1994, SAIHO-JI WAS NEVER MEANT TO BE A GARDEN COVERED IN MOSS. SOSEKI PLANNED TWO SECTORS, A DRY LANDSCAPE SECTION AND A CIRCLING "GOLDEN" POND DESIGNED TO REPRESENT THE JAPANESE CHARACTER FOR "SPIRIT". SCATTERED AROUND THIS POND ARE PAVILIONS INTERLOCKING WITH BRIDGES AND PATHWAYS. ONCE THE GARDEN WAS BUILT HOWEVER, NATURE TOOK CONTROL AND NOW THIS LUSH MAGNIFICENT LANDSCAPE IS RESPLENDENT WITH MOSSES AND LICHEN OF EVERY HUE.

The view of Saiho-ji Temple, Kyoto, in late autumn: the view of the beautiful red leaves falling onto the deep green moss bathed with the morning dew is heavenly.

This moist and glossy moss garden in the rainy season also has a unique, mystical charm as if we had strayed into a mysterious garden; yet the sight of the changing leaves with all their passions, russet with autumn and falling without changing their colours, has a charm like no other, just like looking at the back of someone who is passionately in love but who walks away holding all his emotions tight within.

A garden could remind us of our unconscious feelings when we walk in it.

It is most extraordinary that a garden founded in ancient Japan, first established more than a thousand years ago and redesigned over 500 years ago, can still evoke these turbulent feelings; that this paradise garden is still this perfect oasis that develops our mind.

A garden can help us embrace our soul.

**YUKO OSHIMA**
CREATIVE DIRECTOR, TJM DESIGN CO. LTD
TOKYO, JAPAN

# KOKYO HIGASHI GYOEN
## TOKYO JAPAN

A 20TH CENTURY MODERN GARDEN, KOKYO HIGASHI GYOEN IS PART OF THE IMPERIAL PALACE AND WAS FIRST OPENED TO THE PUBLIC IN 1968. EXTENDING FROM THE *HONMARU* OR PRINCIPLE COMPOUND, THE GARDENS COVER MORE THAN 200,000 SQUARE METRES AND INCLUDE THE *NINOMARU* (SECOND COMPOUND) AND PART OF THE *SANNOMARU* (THE THIRD COMPOUND) OF EDO CASTLE. THE PRINCIPLE COMPOUND COMPRISES A HUGE MANICURED LAWN WHILE THE SECOND COMPOUND IS STRUCTURED VERY MUCH AS AN EDO PERIOD (1603-1868) JAPANESE GARDEN AND, A MUSASHINO COPSE. PERFECTLY GROOMED, THE HIGHLIGHTS OF THE GARDEN ARE DURING THE SPRING MONTHS WHEN THE *SAKURA* OR CHERRY BLOSSOMS ARE IN ALL THEIR GLORY.

Highways beneath like flowing rivers
Cars like gentle fish gliding swiftly along these rivers
The slanting rays of the morning sun are diffused over these rivers, and the shadows of the buildings of sleepy downtown Tokyo resemble massive rocks of different sizes edged along these rivers.
With the increasing brightness of the rising sun, the shapes of the huge rocks slowly transform themselves into buildings with their various functions
Small stones, once hidden and invisible in the shadows of these huge rocks formed by the oblique morning sun, start to sparkle.
These sparkling small stones slowly become the rooftops of houses of city dwellers.

The highways and buildings when shadowed by the "mist" when sunlight was absent reveal scenery akin to the mountains and rivers of Guilin (China) as in an oriental watercolour.
This interplay of sunshine under the changing climatic conditions of the four seasons creates many different shades of scenery.

This is our Tokyo garden seen from a height.

**JUNKO KOSHINO**
FASHION DESIGNER
TOKYO, JAPAN

# KAIRAKU-EN

## MITO, IBARAKI JAPAN

KAIRAKU-EN IS A 19TH CENTURY STROLL GARDEN BUILT BY NARIAKAI TOKUGAWA, THE FEUDAL LORD OF MITO. LAID ACROSS 31 ACRES, IT IS KNOWN AS ONE OF THE "THREE CELEBRATED GARDENS" OF JAPAN. DURING SPRING, WHEN THE MORE THAN 100 SPECIES AND THOUSANDS OF PLUM AND CHERRY BLOSSOM TREES BLOOM, THE GARDEN IS FILLED WITH SPECTATORS. ITS CLEVER DESIGN MAKES GREAT USE OF ITS SURROUNDING FEATURES, INCLUDING LAKE SENBA WHICH IS USED AS ITS POND. KAIRAKU-EN MEANS "GARDEN TO BE ENJOYED BY THE PEOPLE" AND KEEPING TRUE TO ITS NAME, TOKUGAWA OPENED THIS GARDEN TO THE PEOPLE FOR THEIR ENJOYMENT. AT THE TIME THIS WAS INDEED A REVOLUTIONARY AND PIONEERING IDEA AND LED, IN THE LONG TERM, TO THE DEVELOPMENT OF NATIONAL PARKS.

In our present age where global warming has become such a serious issue, I think what people want is not so much to build more buildings as to have more greenery and create gardens which are inspired by thoughts in harmony with nature, something our ancestors valued but contemporary capitalism has forgotten.

Every time I travel in Asia, and every time I stand in an Asian garden and take a deep breath, I feel, with all my senses, the original harmony of human beings and nature; this was not something unilaterally designed by human beings based on their own powers and political ideals. It is that part of our human nature that is surpassingly beautiful, truly and deeply involved in nature itself and under no constraints. The sight of a diversity of flowers in bloom intermingling daringly, delicately and lovingly speaks to the bottom of our heart—"human beings, who are part of nature, should also be like this." I think we should cherish this sight and use it as our model in creating a garden and building the earth as well as a nation, since you can get glimpses of the great wisdom of nature and the human beings in it.

I would like to congratulate the authors of the publication *Paradise Found*. I wholeheartedly wish that this book will not merely be appreciated but also become an important guide as we enter a new era.

**AMON MIYAMOTO**
STAGE DIRECTOR
TOKYO, JAPAN

# DISTINGUISHED CONTRIBUTING WRITERS

It is the eloquent words, the personal reflections and the insightful thoughts of these well-known and distinguished contributing guest writers that have made it possible for all who read this book to make this journey through these Noble Gardens of Asia. It is their sentiments which bring each of these unique Edens closer to all of us. The Chelsea Pensioners' Appeal and the Book Committee are beholden to the following *(by order of appearance in the book)*:-

**Julian Dowle (Introduction) pp. 12-14**—With 35 years experience in landscape design, including 11 Gold Medals at the Chelsea Flower Show, Julian Dowle does work ranging from the design and management of large country gardens to small urban spaces, commercial design, consultancy, lecturing and international judging, throughout the UK, Europe, USA, Japan, Australia and New Zealand. Julian is a holder of the highly prestigious Royal Horticulture Society Veitch Memorial Medal, awarded to people who have made an outstanding contribution to the advancement and improvement of the science and practice of horticulture.

**Mitchell Abdul Karim Crites (South Asia Introduction) pp. 21-22**—A respected scholar and author who has travelled extensively the Arab world and India. He is the leading force for the renaissance of traditional Islamic and Indian craftsmanship and has worked for more than 35 years for the restoration and recognition of these precious skills. He has lectured on Islamic Art at the British Museum and Sotheby's, and has led tours of gardens and architecture in India with British garden designer Penelope Hobhouse. Inspired by the beauty of the Taj Mahal, he decided to create a company, Saray, that would promote and protect the artistic heritage of traditional cultures from Morocco to Malaysia. He designed the white marble Jasmine Garden for the Water Palace in Jaipur and has recently published *India Sublime: Princely Palace Hotels of Rajasthan*. Crites maintains an art gallery, residences and workshops in London, Delhi and Jaipur.

**Durdana Soomro (Wah Gardens) p. 27**—Author of *Karachi: Pleasure Gardens of a Raj City* (2007). The book is an account of Karachi's private and public gardens and offers a rare glimpse into a little known aspect of this former colonial city. Durdana grew up in Bangladesh and also co-authored with her sister Ghazala Hameed, *Bengal Raag*. She is editor of the magazine of the Horticultural Society of Pakistan and has contributed articles and photographs to various English language newspapers. An accomplished linguist, she has translated many published texts from Urdu into English. Durdana has an MBA from Punjab University and an MA in Near and Middle Eastern Studies from the School of Oriental and African Studies, London. She lives in Karachi and is an avid golfer.

**Professor James L. Wescoat, Jr. (Jahangir's Tomb Garden) pp. 28-30**—Professor and Head of the Department of Landscape Architecture at the University of Illinois at Urbana-Champaign, Professor Wescoat's research focuses on water in environmental design in South Asia and the United States. He co-directed the Smithsonian Institution's "Mughal Garden Project" in Lahore, Pakistan from 1986 to 1996 with colleagues in the Pakistan Department of Archaeology and the University of Engineering and Technology-Lahore. Over the past decade he has worked on cultural landscape heritage projects in Agra, Gujarat, and Rajasthan, India; and in 2007 he co-organised "Three Shalamar Baghs Conservation Workshop" with colleagues from Delhi, Lahore, and Srinagar—cities that have a shared Mughal garden heritage, each also having a famous garden known as Shalimar.

**Yasmeen Lari (Hiran Minar, Sheikhupura Fort) pp. 32-34**—The first woman architect in Pakistan. After attending the Oxford School of Architecture, Yasmeen returned to Pakistan with her husband and opened Lari Associates in Karachi. She was president of the Institute of Architects in Pakistan from 1980 to 1983 and is heavily involved in the preservation of historical buildings, monuments, and cities in Pakistan. In line with this, she founded the Heritage Foundation to advocate the documentation and preservation of historical sites and buildings. In 2002 the Heritage Foundation received the Recognition Award from the UN System in Pakistan for its efforts and results. Yasmeen Lari is also the chairperson of the Karavan Initiatives and works extensively in humanitarian efforts.

**Professor Azim Nanji (Shalimar Bagh) pp. 36-39**—A Director of the Institute of Ismaili Studies in London since 1998, Professor Azim Nanji was previously Professor and Chair of the Department of Religion at the University of Florida and has held academic and administrative appointments at various American and Canadian universities. In 2004 he was a visiting Professor at Stanford University. He has authored, co-authored and edited several books including: *The Nizari Ismaili Tradition* (1976), *The Muslim Almanac* (1996), *Mapping Islamic Studies* (1997), *The Historical Atlas of Islam* (with M. Ruthven) (2004) and the *Historical Dictionary of Islam* (Penguin 2008). He also served as the Associate Editor of the new edition of the 15-volume *Encyclopedia of Religion* (Thomson/Gale 2005).

**H.H. Maharajah of Kashmir, Dr. Karan Singh (Shalimar Bagh) p. 43**—First entered politics when he was appointed Regent in 1949 by his father on the intervention of Prime Minister Jawaharlal Nehru. He was the head of the Indian State of Jammu & Kashmir for the next eighteen years as Regent, as elected Sadar-i-Riyasat and lastly as Governor. In 1967, Dr. Karan Singh was inducted as a member of the Union Cabinet headed by Prime Minister Indira Gandhi. At 36, he was the youngest Central Cabinet Minister in India and was soon elected to the Lok Sabha. He is now a member of the Rajya Sabha (the Upper House of Parliament) from New Delhi. During his illustrious career he has served as Minister of Tourism and Civil Aviation, Minister of Health and Family Planning and Minister of Education and Culture. His charitable trusts include the Hari-Tara Charitable Trust and the Dharmarth Trust amongst many. He has also held positions as University Chancellor, Chairman and President of various foundations and government and non-governmental institutions and has written a number of books on political science, religion, philosophical essays, travelogues and poetry. His Amar Mahal Palace has been converted into a Museum and Library.

**Elizabeth Hurley (Nishat Bagh) p. 46**—Elizabeth Hurley lives between London, Gloucestershire and Bombay with her five-year-old son Damian, her husband Arun Nayar and an assortment of animals. She earns her living by acting, modelling, farming and designing beachwear. Elizabeth started her career as an actress and has made more than two dozen movies to date. Her personal favorites are *Austin Powers* and *Bedazzled*. She also produced several movies starring her former boyfriend, Hugh Grant —*Extreme Measures* and *Mickey Blue Eyes*. Elizabeth has been under contract to Estée Lauder for the past thirteen years, making it one of the world's longest running beauty contracts. She has just signed up for a further two years. Every October she tours the United States and other parts of the world raising funds and awareness for The Breast Cancer Research Foundation. In April 2005, Elizabeth launched Elizabeth Hurley Beach. It is now available in numerous high-end boutiques and department stores throughout the world and also at Elizabethhurley.com. Elizabeth was voted Entrepreneur of the Year 2006, by *Glamour* Magazine. She recently launched beachwear for kids. Elizabeth owns a 400-acre farm in Gloucestershire, where she is developing a line of organic food.

**Vikram Lall (The Rock Garden Chandigarh) pp. 48-51**—A world renown architect, Vikram received his Bachelor of Architecture from Chandigarh College of Architecture and a Master of Studies on Interdisciplinary Design for the Built Environment from the University of Cambridge, UK. He is currently a partner & principal architect of Lall & Associates. For twenty years design teams led by Vikram have successfully completed over 250 projects of which many have received critical acclaim. He is a member of the Council of Architecture, India, the Indian Institute of Architecture, the India Habitat Centre and the Indian National Trust for Art and Cultural Heritage. Vikram is also actively involved in publishing, lecturing and research as well as being a visiting faculty & jury to the School of Planning & Architecture, TVB School of Habitat Studies at New Delhi. He has been honoured by the President of India for his work in Urban Design as well as by the Governor of Bihar for the Schematic Conjecture of the Ancient City of Pataliputra.

**Hon. James Curzon (Humayun's Tomb Garden) pp. 52-55**—The Hon. James Curzon is a landowner and historian. The youngest of four sons, he was brought up in the Neo-Classical splendour of his ancestral home Kedleston Hall in Derbyshire. His late father, 3rd Viscount Scarsdale, the nephew of Lord Curzon (Viceroy of India 1899-1905), gave the house to the National Trust in perpetuity in 1987. James bought back the estate in 2006 and as co-owner of Kedleston Estate is currently restoring the lodge and its gardens. Educated at Eton, he graduated from the University of Edinburgh with a Masters degree in History of Art. James has travelled extensively in Asia and the Far East. He has previously written about Lord Curzon and the Delhi Durbar of 1903 to mark its centenary in 2003 for the Royal Oak Foundation. His lifelong love of fine architecture in its historic landscape setting is a constant inspiration to him. He is deeply grateful to be asked to contribute to this wonderfully illustrated book for such a deserving cause which will give one of London's oldest and finest landmarks a new lease of life.

**H.H. Princess Madhavi Scindia, Rajmata of Gwalior** (Sahelion-ki-Bari) **p. 58**—Her Highness is a princess of Nepal and the Maharani of Gwalior, widow of the late Maharajah of Gwalior, Madhavrao Scindia, an internationally well-known charismatic leader and seasoned politician (former Minister of Railways, Aviation and Human Resource & Development and Deputy Leader of the Congress Party) who died tragically in 2001 in a plane crash. Described as one of the most beautiful women in India, the Rajmata has traveled the length and breadth of India and the world with her late husband. Her knowledge and appreciation of Indian gardens and flowers is reflected in the beautiful gardens of her own palace Jai Vilas in Gwalior. Her Highness is an artist and paints portraits, landscapes and flowers. Her Highness loves flowers and is an adept floral decoration expert. The Rajmata has two children and 4 grandchildren. Her son and current Maharajah, H.H. Jyotiraditya Scindia, is a graduate of Harvard, with an MBA from Stanford, and is one of the youngest Members of the Indian Parliament. Her daughter, Princess Chitrangada, who is fond of sports and riding and an accomplished artist, is married to Prince Vikram Singh, the eldest son of Dr. Karan Singh, the Maharajah of Kashmir.

**Sunita Kohli** (Theosophical Garden) **pp. 60-62**—Research-based interior designer, architectural restorer and furniture manufacturer, Sunita has worked throughout the world. She specialises in the design of public buildings, hotels and resorts, forts, palaces, heritage properties, corporate offices and private residences. She has also designed luxury hotel boats on the river Nile and the interiors of official aircraft. Notably, she has restored and decorated Rashtrapati Bhawan (previously Viceroy's House) in New Delhi. In 1992, she was conferred the first 'Padma Shri' by the President of India "for contribution to national life by excellence in the field of Interior Design and Architectural Restoration". With a colleague, she coordinated the design and execution of the Memorial to the late Prime Minister Rajiv Gandhi in Sriperumbudur in South India. In 2005, she founded the Museum of Women in the Arts, India. Sunita has been a guest lecturer at Harvard and Emory Universities, and at the National Building Museum in Washington D.C., amongst others. She has published several papers and is working on books on *Sir Edwin Lutyens and New Delhi*, *Tanjore Paintings*, *Mughal Jewellery*, *Awadhi Cuisine* and a *Children's book on Delhi's Architecture*. She is a Fellow of the RSA in England and of the Halle Institute of Global Learning at Emory University in Atlanta, USA.

**Datin Shalini Amerasinghe Ganendra** (Royal Botanic Gardens, Peradeniya) **pp.64-66**—Datin Shalini was born in Sri Lanka. She now resides in Kuala Lumpur, Malaysia, with her husband and three children and heads the fine arts consultancy and gallery, Shalini Ganendra Fine Art. In 2007, she established the gallery's presence in London. She is President of the Oxford & Cambridge Society, Malaysia, and a founding member of the English Speaking Union, Malaysia. Datin Shalini graduated from Phillips Exeter Academy, USA, where she recently became a Harkness Fellow. She read law at Trinity Hall, Cambridge University, and completed postgraduate legal study at Columbia University Law School. She is a qualified New York attorney and Barrister at law. She practiced international corporate finance with a Wall Street firm in New York before pursuing her vocation in fine arts. Her grandfather, Henry Ashmore Pieris, was an advisor to the Peradeniya Gardens in the 1930's, as a member of the Ceylon civil service. He was the first Sri Lankan Divisional Agriculture officer of Kandy.

**George Alagiah, OBE** (The Brief Garden) **p. 71**—The Presenter of the BBC's prime-time Six O'clock News and World News Today on its global channel, BBC World. Before going behind the studio desk, Alagiah was one of the BBC's leading foreign correspondents reporting on some of the most significant events of the last decade and a half including: the plight of the Kurdish population under Saddam Hussein, the civil war and famine in Somalia, the genocide in Rwanda and the conflicts in Afghanistan, Liberia and Sierra Leone to name but a few. His work has been recognized by the Monte Carlo Television Festival, the Royal Television Society, the British Academy of Film and Television Arts, Amnesty International, the James Cameron Memorial Trust and he was part of the BBC team which collected a BAFTA in 2000 for its coverage of the Kosovo conflict. He is patron of the Fairtrade Foundation and a Governor of the Royal Shakespeare Company. As an author his works include the award-winning *A Passage To Africa* and *A Home from Home*. To cap this illustrious career, Alagiah was awarded the OBE in the 2008 Queen's New Year's Honours List for his services to journalism.

**Dr. Kiat W. Tan** (South East Asian Introduction) **pp. 75-76**—Dr. Tan is the Advisor to the National Parks Board of Singapore. Dr. Tan was born in Singapore, and received his tertiary education in the USA and completed his Ph.D in Biology at the University of Miami, Florida. An orchid specialist, Dr. Tan was the Assistant Director of the Marie Selby Botanical Gardens in Florida. He became Director of the Singapore Botanic Gardens in 1988, Commissioner of Parks and Recreation in 1995, and CEO of the National Parks Board in 1996. Dr. Tan serves as a Trustee of the World Orchid Conference Trust, and is the Project Director for Singapore's new Gardens by the Bay.

**Dr. Woraphat Arthayukti** (Queen Sirikit Botanic Garden) **pp. 78-80**—A Senior Associate of the Kenan Institute Asia and former Vice Chairman of the Friendship to Community Foundation, and Manager of the Cornerstone Asia Project at Kenan Institute Asia. He was previously Vice President, Public Affairs, Unocal Thailand Ltd., and prior to that, served in government as an officer in the Royal Thai Army attached to the Office of the Permanent Secretary of the Ministry of Defence, and as Associate Professor and Head of the Department of Chemical Engineering, Chulangkorn University in Bangkok. He was Deputy Director at the Petroleum and Petrochemical College when he left government service. Dr. Woraphat has also served as Honorary Secretary of The Siam Society under Royal Patronage as well as a board member of the Hornbill Research Foundation and of TTL Co., Ltd., and Chairman of the American Institute of Chemical Engineers, Thailand Club. He has received several royal decorations including Knight Grand Cross (First Class) of the Most Noble Order of the Crown of Thailand and Knight Commander (Second class) of the Most Exalted Order of the White Elephant.

**H.E. Mr. Nitya Pibulsonggram** (Nong Nooch Tropical Botanical Garden) **p. 85**—Minister of Foreign Affairs of the Royal Kingdom of Thailand. His Excellency's impeccable pedigree and exemplary work for Thailand includes having been Advisor to the Minister of Foreign Affairs, Chief Negotiator for the Thai-U.S. Free Trade Agreement, Permanent Secretary of the Ministry of Foreign Affairs, Permanent Representative of Thailand to the United Nations in New York and Ambassador Extraordinary and Plenipotentiary of Thailand to the United States. Among his many decorations are the Grand Companion of the Most Illustrious Order of Chula Chom Klao, Knight Grand Cross (First Class) of the Most Exalted Order of the White Elephant, Knight Grand Cordon (Special Class) of the Most Noble Order of the Crown of Thailand and King Bhumibol Adulyadej's Royal Cypher Medal (Rama IX).

**Dato' Professor Jimmy Choo, OBE** (The Lake Garden / Taman Tasik Perdana) **p. 89**—A London-based luxury fashion designer best known for his exquisite hand-made women's shoes, Jimmy Choo is a Malaysian of Hakka Chinese descent who was born in Penang into a family of shoemakers. He is perhaps the most famous of the alumni of Cordwainers' Technical College in London, from which he graduated in 1983. Choo's humble beginnings can be traced back to his workshop in Hackney, East London, which he opened in 1986 by renting an old hospital building. His craftsmanship and designs soon became noticed and he came to international fame when his creations were featured in a record eight pages in a 1988 issue of *Vogue* magazine. Patronage from Diana, Princess of Wales from 1990 onwards further boosted his image. In 1996, he co-founded Jimmy Choo Ltd. with UK *Vogue* accessories editor Tamara Mellon. Choo now resides chiefly in London. He is involved in a project to set up a shoe-making institute in his country of birth Malaysia, where his iconic status is often evoked to inspire budding shoemakers and fashion designers.

**H.H. Prince Abdullah, Tunku Panglima Besar, Negeri Sembilan** (Putrajaya Botanical Garden / Taman Botani Putrajaya) **p. 92**—The son of Malaysia's first post-Independence King and one of Malaysia's founding fathers, His Highness actively served in the civil service for more than 10 years before being involved in politics. He was the member for Parliament in Rawang Constituency from 1964 to 1974 whilst presiding in several voluntary organisations such as the Malaysian Association of Youth Clubs (1954-1970), the Malaysian Youth Council (1966-1972), the Asian Youth Council (1972-1978), and was also an executive member of the World Assembly of Youth. Moving into the private sector, His Highness founded the Melewar Corporation, a family-run business conglomerate whose interests range from education to insurance, travel and tourism to television. He is also the Chairman of several public-listed companies including MAA Holdings Berhad and the Melewar Industrial Group Berhad. A family man, he is the father of 9 children.

**Y. Bhg Dato' Seri Tengku Datuk (Dr.) Zainal Adlin, Ph.D** (Sabah Agriculture Park / Taman Pertanian Sabah) **pp. 94-97**—Chairman of the Sabah Tourism Board and Executive Chairman of Triomac Engineering Sdn. Bhd. Tengku Adlin is Vice President Emeritus/Past Chairman of the World Wide Fund for Nature (WWF) Malaysia and was a member of the Board of Trustees of WWF-International, Chairman of the Danum Valley Management Committee, Chairman Sabah Wetlands Conservation Society, Chairman Outward Bound Sabah, Honorary Vice President Raleigh International, U.K., and Honorary Member of the Scientific Exploration Society, U.K., among others. He served as a pilot in the late fifties and early sixties before following a career in the civil service for 34 years. He was Chief Executive Officer of the Sabah State Housing Commission and the Deputy Director of the Sabah Foundation until the mid-nineties; and was responsible for the institutional and capacity building of the two statutory bodies. He has also written books and publications on nature and adventure, having led or participated in many expeditions to the unexplored or lesser known parts of Sabah since the late sixties.

**Christina Ong** (Singapore Botanic Gardens) **p. 101**—Chairman of the National Parks Board of Singapore and Managing Director of Club 21 Pte. Ltd., Mrs. Ong is a lifestyle retailer with more than 200 stores worldwide. A leading fashion entrepreneur, Mrs. Ong is a recipient of The Italian Fashion Hall of Fame Award in 1995 and the Italian Award of Cavaliere De Lavo. Mrs. Ong is also a noted luxury hotelier, managing a stable of niche properties under the COMO Hotels brand.

**Dr. Henry Oakeley** (National Orchid Garden, Singapore Botanic Gardens) **pp. 102-105**—President of the Orchid Society of Great Britain and (until recently) Chairman of the RHS Orchid Committee, Dr. Oakeley has been growing orchids for 50 years, and his particular interest is in Lycaste, Ida and Anguloa orchids from Latin America. He is also the Garden Fellow, Royal College of Physicians of London (where he supervises the medicinal plant garden); Honorary Research Associate in Orchid Science, Royal Botanic Gardens, Kew; Honorary Research Associate, Singapore Botanic Gardens; Chairman of the Lycaste Club of Japan, and holder of the National Collection of Lycaste, Ida and Anguloa.

**Aileen T. Lau** (Kranji War Cemetery) **p. 108**—Editor of *Oriental Art*, a scholarly journal established in 1948, dedicated to Asian art history. She is also an editor and publisher of books in the field of nature, heritage, history and Chinese ceramics, under the Suntree imprint. Among her works, she has authored *Gateway*, a book on polytechnic education at a local institution, and *Birds Seen at the Istana*, as well as edited and contributed to others like *Gardens of the Istana* and *Maritime Heritage of Singapore*. She is a Committee Member of the Orchid Society of South East Asia and a member of the Singapore Gardening Society. She is also President of The China Society and much involved in cultural activities and studies. She enjoys tending her orchids and has been a bird watcher over the past 18 years.

**Benny Ong** (Singapore Zoological Gardens) **p. 112**—A veteran of the fashion and textiles business who, in the past thirty years, has established a global brand name. His prestigious list of clients includes Queen Noor of Jordan, the Duchess of Kent, and the Late Princess of Wales. He supplies to almost all leading retail stores from Bergdorf Goodman in New York to Harrods in London. The rich heritage and tradition of textiles in South East Asia has constantly inspired him. His 'rediscovery' of the wonderful legacies of colours, designs and artistic skills of the peoples of Indochina encouraged him to revive their fading traditions and to bring its charms to the world. He created a social enterprise that crosses geographic borders, the Council of Weavers. Benny envisions in his future the creation of an international foundation based upon his philosophies and his love for life, and which will champion humanitarian, social and cultural causes. In 2007, Benny was invited by the Singapore Arts Museum to present a retrospective of his artworks. His remarkable show, *REWOVEN*, represents Benny's journey from fashion designer to artist and has run from November 2007.

**Professor Dr. Umar Anggara Jenie** (Bogor Botanic Gardens / Taman Sari Kebun Raya) **pp. 114-117**—Chairman of the Indonesian Institute of Sciences and a Professor of Organic Medicinal Chemistry of the Gadjah Mada University (Indonesia). He has worked on various UNESCO panels with specific reference to Bioethics and Human Rights and also serves as Chairman of the National Bioethics Commission. He is a member of the Indonesian Academy of Sciences, the National Research Council (Indonesia), and the Educational Section of the Indonesian Association of Pharmaceutical Sciences amongst many others. Professor Jenie received a Ph.D in Chemistry from the Australian National University (Australia) and undertook post-doctorate training and research at Osaka University (Japan), University of Newcastle (U.K.) and Xing-hua University (Taiwan).

**Anak Agung Gede Dharma Widoere Djelantik** (Tirtagangga) **p. 118-121**—Chairman of Tirtagangga, Prince Widoere is from the Royal family of Karangasem. His grandfather, the last Raja of Karangasem, was an architect and lecturer and built several water gardens including Tirtagangga. Prince Widoere studied in Holland and has worked as a development engineer throughout the world. Currently the Prince is senior advisor to Staatsbosbeheer, the Dutch forestry department.

**Made Wijaya** (Villa Bebek) **p. 124**—Australian-born Made Wijaya or Michael White arrived in Bali, Indonesia in 1973 after jumping ship and swimming ashore for what was meant to be a break from Architectural College. After working as a tourist guide, tennis coach and photo-journalist and living with a Balinese Brahman family for six years, he had become Made Wijaya and was asked to design the gardens of the Bali Hyatt. Now, with more than 1000 tropical gardens to his name and a work force of over 300, Made Wijaya is known as the leading contemporary exponent of exotic garden design. His work can be seen largely through South East Asia and India, but also in southern Europe and the Caribbean. He has written seven books on tropical landscape and architectural design.

**Professor Paulo Alcazaren** (Makiling Botanic Gardens) **pp. 126-128**—A Professor at the University of Philippines, Professor Alcazaren is a prolific author and writes a popular column on urbanism and design for the *Philippine Star*, a Manila broadsheet. He is a founding member of the country's Heritage Conservation Society and is active in various civil-society groups. He is editor-in-chief of *BluPrint Magazine*, a design magazine, and an established architectural photographer. As an urban designer and landscape architect, Paulo has designed over 200 projects including parks, plazas, campuses and resorts that have taken him to 12 countries in South East Asia, China and the Middle East. He has received awards for his journalism and advocacy in the Philippines as well as honours in that country and Singapore for his landscape and urban design.

**Evangelina Lourdes "Luli" M. Arroyo** (Malacañan Palace Grounds) **pp. 130-133**—The daughter of President Gloria Macapagal-Arroyo of the Philippines. Graduating from the Ateneo de Manila University with a degree in Management Economics, she earned a Master of Science in Foreign Service (MSFS) from Georgetown University, Washington D.C. Luli is currently regional policy officer at the World Wide Fund for Nature for the Coral Triangle Initiative, covering South East Asia and the Pacific Islands. A writer, researcher and analyst active in public policy, Luli was a consultant for the Philippines government during the APEC Summit in Manila in 1996, a senior staffer for her mother in the Philippines Senate from 1997 to 1998, and from that time until 2007 she was Program Officer of the Philippine Foundation for Global Concerns (PFGC) and Director for Strategic Development of the Foundation for Information Technology Education & Development (FIT-ED) in Manila. Luli lives with her parents at Malacañan Palace, the official residence of the President of the Philippines.

**Professor Tadashi Yokoyama** (East Asia Introduction) **pp. 137-138**—President of the Institute of Advanced Media Arts and Sciences and Professor Emeritus of the University of Tokyo, Professor Yokoyama specialises in the History of Space (Architecture/Garden) Organisation. His academic tomes include *European Gardens—History, Space Organization and Design* (Tokyo 1988), *Box as a Theatre (Concept of Box in the Contemporary Art)* (Tokyo 1989), *Strolling the World of Sukiya* (Tokyo 1997), as well as editing and writing for *Zen and Architecture/Garden* (Tokyo 2002). Born in Gifu City, he graduated from the Graduate School of Architecture at the University of Tokyo from which he retired as a Professor in 2000. He has also written for the cultural heritage protection office of UNESCO including 'Between Artificiality and Nature' in *Gardens and their Environmental Context*.

**Kai-Yin Lo** (Hong Kong Zoological & Botanical Gardens) **p. 143**—Internationally acclaimed as a jewellery and accessories designer and the recipient of the prestigious World's Outstanding Chinese Designer, 2007 award from the Hong Kong Design Centre. Described by the *Wall Street Journal* as a "Renaissance Woman", Kai-Yin is an expert and consultant on aspects of Asian arts and culture, and a speaker on Chinese history, heritage and broad issues of design and the creative industries. She has edited and co-edited four books on Chinese culture. Her latest, *House, Home, Family: Living and Being Chinese* has been adopted as a text by over 20 universities in the USA in their Asian Studies course. She was honoured alongside Cartier as one of three jewellers lauded for their "influence, style and excellence" by the Kennedy Center and has worked with a host of others including Sotheby's London, World Wildlife Fund and Shanghai Tang. She is the only jewellery designer to have been honoured with stamps by China's Post Office. Kai-Yin is a Visiting Professor at the Academy of Arts and Design, Tsinghua University, Beijing, a member of the Asia-Pacific Art Acquisition Committee of the Tate and the International council of the Asia Society, as well as being the curator of the Hong Kong Heritage Museum's exhibition on jewellery design.

**Nora Sun** (Yu Yuan) **p. 146**—The granddaughter of the Republic of China's founding father Dr. Sun Yat-Sen, Nora Sun is the president of a consulting firm, Nora Sun Associates Ltd. specialising in business formation and government relations in mainland China. She has also served as Principal Commercial Officer in the U.S. consulates in Shanghai and Guangzhou. During her diplomatic assignments in the mainland, Nora Sun facilitated major U.S. investments as well as assisted in resolving issues for U.S. companies. Sun was later appointed by the U.S. government to serve as commercial attaché in the U.S. embassy in France.

**Professor Pan, Gong-Kai** (Liu Yuan) **p. 151**—President of the Central Academy of Fine Arts, a renowned traditional Chinese painter and art philosopher, Professor Pan has served as Dean at two of the most influential art academies in China. Ever since the 1980's, his academic proposition that called for a "mutually complementing and enriching" tie between Oriental and Western art systems has had a substantial influence on China's art community. His personal exhibitions have been showcased at the Phillips Gallery in Soho, New York; the Chinese Culture Center of San Francisco; the Art Gallery of the Sino-Japan Friendship Association in Tokyo; the UNESCO Headquarters in Paris; art museums all over China; and many other prominent places. His publications include: *The History of Paintings in China, Restriction and Expansion, An Analysis of Pan Tianshou's Painting Techniques, A Critical Biography of Pan Tianshou.* He is also editor-in-chief of the *Modern Design* series and *A Collection of Pan Tianshou's Paintings and Calligraphies,* both of which were awarded the National Book Prize. In recent years, he has been conducting research on and writing about *The Road of Chinese Modern Art.*

**Sir David Tang** (Ji Chang Yuan) **p. 155**—Born in Hong Kong, Sir David is a member of the fourth generation of Cantonese refugees. The family was Buddhist in faith, but he was baptised in order to attend the local Catholic school La Salle. He was then sent off to boarding school in England. He read Philosophy at university and went to Law College. In 1983-84, he taught at Peking University. He is passionate about things Chinese and is the founder of the China Club in Hong Kong, Peking and Singapore; and Shanghai Tang, and recently, China Tang in London. His other businesses have involved oil exploration, gold mining, cigars and consultancy to multinationals and international brands. He seems to have lived mostly on British Airways between London and Hong Kong, but since turning 50 in 2004, chooses to stay at home in Hong Kong as much as possible with his family and 4 dogs, playing the piano, completing the daily cryptic crossword, and reading voraciously.

**Yang, Lan** (Imperial Gardens Jing Shan Gong Yuan including Bei Hai Park, Beijing) **p. 158**—Chairperson of Sun Media Group and Sun Culture Foundation, Ms. Yang is also a leading television anchor in China. She is the co-founder of Sun Media Investment Holdings Ltd., whose businesses include television production, newspapers and magazines, and on line publishing. In 2005, she founded Sun Culture Foundation to promote the relief of poverty, advancement of education, and mutual understanding across cultures. A graduate of Beijing Foreign Studies University, she went on to complete her Masters in International Affairs from Columbia University. In 1999 and 2001, Ms. Yang was named by *Asiaweek* magazine as one of the "Leaders in Society and Culture in Asia" and one of the "Movers and Shapers of the 21st Century China". She also received the Chinese Women of the Year award in 2001 and Top Ten Women Entrepreneurs award in 2002. She actively serves as goodwill ambassador for several national charity foundations, promoting environmental protection, education, blood donation, and also for the 2008 Olympic Games. She is a member of the 10th National Committee of the Chinese People's Political Consultative Conference (CPPCC) and of the Columbia University International Advisory Council (IAC).

**Chung, Myung-Whun** (Soswaewon Garden) **p. 162**—Principal Conductor of the Seoul Philharmonic Orchestra. In 2000 he took responsibility for the musical direction of the Orchestra Philharmonique de Radio France. He has appeared as guest conductor with virtually every great orchestra, including the Berlin and Vienna Philharmonics, the London, Boston and Chicago Symphony Orchestras, the Cleveland Orchestra, the Royal Concertgebouworkest Orchestra, the Metropolitan Opera Orchestra, the New York Philharmonic, the Philadelphia Orchestra and the Philharmonia Orchestra. In addition to being awarded numerous music prizes, Chung, Myung-Whun is deeply sensitive to humanitarian and ecological problems of our age, and has devoted an important part of his life to these causes. In 1994 he launched a series of musical and environmental projects in Korea for youth. He served as Ambassador for the Drug Control Programme at the United Nations (UNDCP). He has also been honoured with Korea's most distinguished cultural award "Kumkwan" and was named Man of the Year by UNESCO.

**Professor Choe, Jae Chun** (Chollipo Arboretum) **p. 167**—University Chair Professor at Ewha Woman's University, Seoul, Director of the Natural History Museum, and Director, Research Institute of EcoScience, Ewha Woman's University. Professor Choe has also been a Research Associate at the American Museum of Natural History since 2006, a Research Associate at Harvard University Museum of Comparative Zoology since 2001, and President of the Ecological Society of Korea. He received his Ph.D from Harvard University and taught at Tufts University and the University of Michigan before returning to Korea. He is an author of numerous articles and books on the ecology and evolution of social behavior and mating systems and, amongst many awards, has received the BPW Gold Award in 2005, the National Decoration of Science and Technology in 2004, The Korean Women's Movement Award in 2004 and the Asian Environmental Award in 2002 for his effort in promoting public awareness of environmental issues through his newspaper columns and public lectures.

**Professor Jung, Young-Sun** (Hee Won Garden, Ho-Am Art Museum) **pp. 168-170**—President of STL (Seoahn Total Landscape) design and consulting group, a firm with a well-established reputation for providing urban design and landscape architectural services of the highest quality to public and private sector clients internationally, including the Hee Won garden at Ho-Am Art Museum. She served as the Director of the Landscape Design Team, Daeneung Engineering, and Professor of the Landscape Architecture Department at Cheongju University. Professor Jung is a graduate from Seoul National University, with a B.A. from the Department of Agriculture and an MLA in Landscape Design from the School of Environmental Studies.

**Professor Dr. Yi, Song-mi** [Changdeokgung (Changdeok Palace)] **pp. 172-174**—Professor Emerita of Art History at the Academy of Korean Studies and an advisor of YEOL, Society for Korea Cultural Heritage. She received her B.A. in Fine Arts at Seoul National University, a M.A. in Art History at U. C. Berkeley, and a Ph.D in Art History at Princeton University. She was Dean of the Graduate School at the Academy, a member of the National History Council of Korea, and also served as President of the Art History Association of Korea. She has published extensively on both Korean and Chinese Art in Korean and English. Her most recent publication in English is *Korean Landscape Painting: Continuity and Innovation through the Ages* (Hollym, 2006).

**Arch. Kengo Kuma** (Byodo-in) **p. 179**—After graduating from the school of engineering at the University of Tokyo in 1979, he moved to New York for further studies at Columbia University in 1985-86. In 1987 he founded the Spatial Design studio and, in 1990, Kengo Kuma & Associates. He has also been a Professor at the faculty of Environmental Information at Keio University, from 1998 to 1999. Kuma's stated goal is to "recover the tradition of Japanese buildings" and to reinterpret it for the 21st century. In 1997 he won the prestigious Architectural Institute of Japan Award.

**Arch. Naoki Terada** (Kinkaku-ji) **pp. 180-183**—Born in Osaka, Japan, he graduated from Meiji University in engineering. He earned his architectural degree in Tokyo, and Architectural Association School of Architecture (AA School) in London. After working in Australia, Italy and Japan, Naoki Terada founded his own design company, Teradadesign, and is also a lecturer at Nihon University, Tokyo.

**Yuko Oshima** (Saiho-Ji) **p. 187**—Graduated from Aoyama University in 1976 and started work with her mother's company, Oshima Hardware Co. Ltd. manufacturing Japanese ship-building hardware and accounting for a 90% share of the Japanese market. In 1985 she established Nova Oshima which introduced contemporary Italian furniture to Japan and held annual exhibitions of Italian designs including those by Ettore Sottsass. In 2005 Nova Oshima merged to become TJM Design Co. Ltd. and Ms. Oshima now works as creative director for the company.

**Junko Koshino** (Kokyo Higashi Gyoen) **p. 190**—An Osaka-born fashion designer. She opened her first boutique in Tokyo in 1966 and 12 years later was showing in Paris. Her label comprises both men and women's wear as well as designs for opera. Sleek colour-blocked sports outfits, distinctive forward-looking corporate and exposition uniforms, costumes of opera fantasy and grandiloquence, and futuristic clothing characterise the work of Junko Koshino. She has had exhibitions at the Metropolitan Museum of Art, N.Y., the National Museum of Chinese History, Beijing, Caroussel du Louvre, Paris, as well as numerous Japanese exhibitions.

**Amon Miyamoto** (Kairaku-en) **p. 194**—Recognised as Japan's foremost director of musicals. With his staging of *Pacific Overtures* (received 4 Tony nominations), he has won great acclaim in the West as well. Currently, Miyamoto is developing projects for the stage in America and England as well as in Japan.

**General Editor: H.H. Princess Soraya Dakhlah**—With more than 15 years in the media industry Soraya has worked throughout South East Asia as a television producer/director and programming director. Today her businesses include publishing and interior design, and she is actively involved in charity work. Soraya is Rear Commodore of the Royal Langkawi Yacht Club and Chairperson of the Royal Langkawi International Regatta.

# ACKNOWLEDGEMENTS

*Paradise Found: Journeys Through Noble Gardens of Asia* would not have been possible without the help and support of so many people all over the world. The Book Project Committee of the Chelsea Pensioners' Appeal would like to thank His Royal Highness, The Prince of Wales, for his support and patronage. It would also like to thank Her Royal Highness, Princess Alexandra, The Honourable Lady Ogilvy, for her kind acceptance to launch the book.

Additionally, the Committee wishes to express its heartfelt gratitude to all Appeal Office staff members at the Royal Hospital Chelsea, and its thanks to all members of the Book Fund-raising Committee for giving so much of their time and effort to the project. In particular, the following are acknowledged for their much appreciated support: General the Lord Walker of Aldringham, Governor of the Royal Hospital Chelsea; the Marquess of Salisbury, Chairman of the Appeal Executive Committee and Sir Ronald Grierson, Chairman of the Book Project Committee.

Finally, the Committee would like to acknowledge and thank all friends and supporters, near and far, who have supported this project in so many different ways. While all should have been remembered and thanked here, sincerest apologies are extended to any who may have been inadvertently overlooked or omitted.

Dato' Abdul Majid Mohammed
Rukhsana Afzaal
Y.M. Tengku Aina Binti Y.T.M Tengku Ismail Shah
Dr. Aleli Agoncillo-Quirante
Marford Angeles
Polly Arber
Jeremy R. Barns
Charlotte Breese
Mike Bruhn
Khadija Buhadi
Radha Burnier
Roberto P. Cereno
Orawan Chaiprom
Datuk Chan, Chew Lun
Jacqui Chan
Chan, Moon Kien
Chan, Ying Lock
Charles Chang
Veronica Tao Chevalier
Dr. Chin, See Chung
Irene Chu
Chung, Soyong
Michele Codoni
Mitchell Abdul Karim Crites
Bernice Croft
Daniela D'Agostino
Department of Agriculture, Sabah
Cedric De Silva
Dooland De Silva
Anak Agung Gede Dharma Widoere Djelantik
Julian Dowle
Julia Elmore
Endang Tjempaka Sari
Evershine Flora Deco
Henry Fan, Hung Ling

Edgar Ryan Faustino
Felix Fong, Wo
Peter Francis
Datin Shalini Amerasinghe Ganendra
Angela Gardner
Lucy George
Helga Haack
Hazman Md Zaki
Heo, Hyun
Irfan Husein
Diane Illavera
Dr. Irawati
Iain Jackson
M. Jojic-Oberoi
Juroting II
Nikhil Khanna
Kim, Min Joo
Kim, Youngja
Kim, Young M'young
Koon Young Klingspor
Tony Lamb
Yasmeen Lari
Victor Lee Fook Choy
Lee, Pin Pin
Lee, So Yeon
Gregory Lepage
Dennis Lim
Anders Lindstrom
Ling, Cheng Lai
Jain Linton
Kai-Yin Lo
Marina Lo
Kay Lyons
Terence F. Mahony
John Maizels
Nitin Mantri

Tony Martin
The Ministry of Agriculture and Food Industries, Sabah
Dr. Weerachai Nanakorn
Natt Haniff
Ng, Lang
Peter O'Connor
Jaseca Oh
Kit Ong
Benny Ong
Yuko Oshima
Alex Peter
S. Harihara Raghavan
Anton Rajer
Roohia Ralhan
Arianna Rinaldo
Nek Chand Saini
Balloo Scholfield
H.H. Jyotiraditya Scindia
H.H. Priyadarshini Raje Scindia
Vivek Sekhar
Putu Semiada
Agus Setiawan
Haji Shahoran Bin Johan Ariffin
Sharif Mahdi Bin Abdul Majid
Sharona Mohamad
H.H. Yuvraj Vikramaditya Singh
H.H. Yuvrani Chitrangada Raje Singh
Ivy Singh-Lim
Siti Zakiah Bt Mohammed
Professor Myonggi Sul
Nora Sun
Tan, Jiew Hoe
Dr. Kiat W. Tan
Mitina Tan
Adeline Tang

Kampon Tansacha
Made Wijaya
Dr. Siril Wijesundera
James Williams
Moses Wong
Dr. Wong, Wei Har
Daisuke Yamamoto
H.H. Tengku Zerafina Idris Shah
Jenny Chan Zurbrugg

*Special thanks to MFX, Kuala Lumpur who have kindly created and prepared artwork and the audio-visual presentation for the launch of this Book. Their support is deeply appreciated.*

### The Book Fund-raising Committee

**Sir Ronald Grierson** (Chairman of the Committee)—A banker and industrialist who has, on several occasions, held full-time appointments in government. He currently chairs the international advisory board of two US businesses, The Blackstone Group and Bain & Co., and is chairman of several international philanthropic bodies in the fields of medicine, education and music.

**Joan Foo Mahony**—A lawyer, publisher, author, sailor and philanthropist who worked in corporate finance in New York, Tokyo and Hong Kong before retiring from legal practice to write, publish, sail and devote her time to various international charities.

**Sarah Williams**—Grew up in India and has lived in Hong Kong. She now resides next door to the Royal Hospital Chelsea. She is deeply involved in wildlife conservation in India and other causes.

# PHOTO CREDITS

**Photo Editor: Natasha O'Connor**—Natasha O'Connor discovered her keen interest in photography while studying for an art history degree at Edinburgh University. This has led her to work with world-class photographers in both editorial & advertising environments. She started her career at Magnum Photos in New York, which then led to working on the Benetton magazine *Colors* in Italy, then back to London where for years she commissioned photography for a leading advertising agency, which has now taken her into a more diverse consulting role.

**Steven Yee Pui Chung**—Founder of PhotoVivo.com and Knowledge Bowl, Steven has established himself as one of Singapore's most prolific and versatile, new generation photographers. Steven's works, many of them influenced by "computer art", have been widely accepted for display at major exhibitions both in Singapore and abroad. These works have garnered numerous awards and honours for the artist. In just three years he has held six solo exhibitions and in 2003, became the youngest person to be admitted to the Fellowship (Applied and Professional Section) of The Royal Photographic Society of Great Britain. In addition, his achievements have been recognised by the International Federation of Photographic Art. Steven's versatility has enabled him to cover a wide range of subjects. By translating them into striking images, he shows a strong desire to communicate his observations to a discerning audience.

**Warrick Page**—Warrick is a native of Melbourne, Australia and graduated from Deakin University with a B.A. in Professional Writing and Journalism in 2003. Since 2004 Warrick has covered breaking news and features in Israel/Palestine, France, Pakistan, Afghanistan and Tajikistan. He was selected for the 2006 Eddie Adams Workshop in Jeffersonville, N.Y. and has been based in Islamabad, Pakistan since November 2004. He contributes regularly to Bloomberg News, Getty Images and Panos Pictures.

**Karena Perronet-Miller**—Anglo-Chilean photographer Karena studied History of Art before travelling extensively throughout the world. She became spellbound with the beauty, history and paradoxes of India years ago and has continued to make India part of her life and creativity. She has photographed India extensively on various commissions and personal projects ranging from 5-star luxury clients to national disasters in the Indian continent for International NGO's and media. She would like to sincerely thank all the team at Indus Tours and travels for the years of support and extensive knowledge and backup on her many trips.

**Helen Kudrich**—Helen Kudrich was originally from Perth, Western Australia and has been based in Bangkok for the past 8 years. Her photography has been exhibited in photographic festivals and galleries internationally, including the Noorderlicht Photo Festival in the Netherlands. Her work has also been published in magazines worldwide—including *Granta*, *Stern*, *Time* and *Global Knowledge*. She recently took part in the *9 Days in the Kingdom* book project—as one of the 55 photographers selected internationally—which commemorates the 80th birthday of the King of Thailand.

**Marc Schlossman**—Marc was born in Chicago and is based in London. From a beginning in editorial photography and photojournalism, he now works using documentary, landscape and photojournalism techniques to explore issues, places and stories around the world. He is a director of Millennium Images and Panos Pictures. He has worked with *The New York Times*, the *Washington Post*, *New Scientist* magazine, Channel 4, Greenpeace, Oxfam and the International Committee of the Red Cross. Marc is co-photographer of two titles in the BBC Books Unforgettable travel book series, *Unforgettable Places* and *Unforgettable Islands*.

**Menchit Ongpin**—Menchit was born in Southern Philippines and earned a degree in Interdisciplinary Studies at the Ateneo de Manila University. She has photographed for most major magazines and newspapers in the Philippines, including *Lifestyle Asia*, *Manila Standard*, *Sense & Style*, *People Asia*, *Philippine Star*, the *Philippine Daily Inquirer*, and the *Manila Bulletin*. She founded Le Studio, a photography company specialising in lifestyle and corporate photography and portraiture. Among her noted portraits are those of former Philippine Presidents Fidel V. Ramos and Corazon Aquino, Senators, artists, society icons and technocrats. Menchit is now based in Hong Kong.

**Daniel Traub**—Daniel is an American photographer and filmmaker, based in China. He has been engaged on a long term basis with *Simplified Characters* which explores the transformation of China's cities through street portraits and urban scenes and a large format series, *City's Edge* which looks at the border region where rural and urban China meet. His images have been exhibited in Asia and the USA, and have been featured in *The New York Times Magazine*, *Telegraph Magazine* and *Wallpaper*.

**Katharina Hesse**—Katharina holds a graduate degree in Chinese (& Japanese) studies from the Institut National des Langues et Civilizations Orientales (INALCO) in Paris; she is one of a few foreign photographers who are accredited by the Ministry of Foreign Affairs and has lived in China for 14 years. Katharina initially worked as an assistant for German TV (ZDF) and then freelanced for *Newsweek* from 1996 to 2002. Her photos have appeared in publications such as *Courrier International*, *Der Spiegel*, *D della Repubblica*, *IO Donna*, *Die Zeit*, *Marie-Claire*, *Neon*, *Newsweek*, *Stern*, *Vanity Fair* (Italian & German editions). Katharina participated in the "A Day in the Life of the American Woman" project in 2005, and won a NPPA 1st prize award in 2003 (Magazine: Portrait & Personality); her work has been featured at photography festivals including Visa Pour l'Image, Perpignan, France and at the Angkor Photo Festival, Cambodia.

**Jean Chung**—After receiving a Master's degree in photojournalism from the University of Missouri in 2003, Jean Chung returned to Seoul to pursue her goal to be an international photojournalist. During her three-year stay in Seoul, she covered various news events and generated photo stories extensively in Asia and the Middle East. She has spent this past year in Kabul, Afghanistan focusing on issues such as education, women's rights, and social changes. On Sept. 6, 2007, she received the Grand Prix Care International du Reportage Humanitaire of Visa Pour L'image Photo Festival in Perpginan, France, for her documentation of maternal mortality in Afghanistan. Her work has been featured in various publications such as *Los Angeles Times*, *Stern*, *Der Spiegel*, *Newsweek*, *New York Times*, *Chicago Tribune*, *Time Asia*, *French GEO*, *Vanity Fair* (Italy) and *Boston Globe*.

**Royal Hospital Chelsea and the Chelsea Pensioners' Appeal** (p. 11)—Courtesy of The Royal Hospital Chelsea.

**PAKISTAN**—**Wah Gardens** (pp. 24-27), **Jahangir's Tomb Garden** [p. 15 (upper right), pp. 18-19, pp. 28-31, pp. 196-197], **Sheikhupura Fort (Hiran Minar)** (pp. 32-35), **Shalimar Bagh** [p. 15 (lower), pp. 36-39]—Warrick Page/Panos Pictures.

**INDIA**—**Shalimar Bagh** (p. 23, pp. 40-43), **Nishat Bagh** [p. 2, pp. 44-46, p. 47 (upper: left & right), p. 208], **The Rock Garden, Chandigarh** (pp. 48-50), **Humayun's Tomb Garden** (pp. 53-55), **Sahelion-ki-Bari** (pp. 56-59), **Theosophical Garden** (pp. 60-63)—Karena Perronet-Miller. **Nishat Bagh** [p. 47 (lower)]—Altaf Qadri/epa/Corbis. **Humayun's Tomb Garden** (p. 52)—Courtesy of the Aga Khan Trust for Culture.

**SRI LANKA**—**Royal Botanic Gardens, Peradeniya** [p. 64, p. 65, p. 66 (left), p. 67 (upper right)]—Courtesy of Datin Shalini Amerasinghe Ganendra; [p. 66 (right), p. 67 (upper left)]—Courtesy of Royal Botanic Gardens, Peradeniya; [p. 67 (lower)]—Getty Images. **The Brief Garden** (pp. 68-71)—Karena Perronet-Miller.

**THAILAND**—**Queen Sirikit Botanic Garden** (pp. 16-17, pp. 78-81), **Nong Nooch Tropical Botanical Garden** [p. 13 (lower left), p. 14 (right), pp. 82-85)]—Helen Kudrich.

**MALAYSIA**—**The Lake Garden/Taman Tasik Perdana** (pp. 86-89), **Putrajaya Botanical Garden/Taman Botani Putrajaya** (pp. 90-93)—Marc Schlossman. **Sabah Agriculture Park/Taman Pertanian Sabah** (pp. 94-97)—Menchit Ongpin.

**SINGAPORE**—**Singapore Botanic Gardens** (p. 6)—Steven Yee/Photovivo.com. **Singapore Botanic Gardens** (pp. 72-73, pp. 98-101), **National Orchid Garden, Singapore Botanic Gardens** (pp. 102-105), **Kranji War Cemetery** (pp. 106-109), **Singapore Zoological Gardens** (pp. 110-113)—Marc Schlossman.

**INDONESIA**—**Bogor Botanic Gardens/Taman Sari Kebun Raya** (pp. 114-117)—Courtesy of Bogor Botanic Gardens; [p. 116 (upper left)]—Photolibrary. **Tirtagangga** (p. 77)—Photolibrary; (pp. 118-121)—Courtesy of Tirtagangga. **Villa Bebek** [p. 122, p. 123, p. 124 (upper left), p. 125 (upper right)]—Courtesy of Made Wijaya; [p. 124 (far left)]—Courtesy of Rio Helmi; [p. 124 (lower left & right), p. 125 (lower left & lower)]—Courtesy of Tim Street Porter.

**PHILIPPINES**—**Makiling Botanic Gardens** [(p. 126, p. 127, p. 128 (left), p. 129 (upper left)]—Courtesy of R.P. Cereno; [p. 128 (centre & right), p. 129 [(upper: centre, right, far right, centre right & lower)]—Menchit Ongpin. **Malacañan Palace Grounds** (p. 130, p. 133)—Courtesy of the Office of the President of the Philippines, Malacañan Palace Museum and Library; (pp. 131-132)—Menchit Ongpin.

**PEOPLE'S REPUBLIC OF CHINA**—**Hong Kong Zoological & Botanical Gardens** (pp. 140-143), **Yu Yuan** (pp. 144-147), **Liu Yuan** (pp. 148-151), **Ji Chang Yuan** (p. 8, pp. 152-155)—Daniel Traub. **Imperial Gardens, Jing Shan Gong Yuan (including Bei Hai Park)** (pp. 156-159)—Katharina Hesse.

**REPUBLIC OF KOREA**—**Soswaewon** [p. 15 (upper left), pp. 160-163], **Chollipo Arboretum** (pp. 164-167), **Hee Won Garden at Ho-Am Art Museum** [p. 13 (upper), p. 139, pp. 168-171], **Changdeokgung (Changdeok Palace)** [p. 14 (left), pp. 172-175]—Jean Chung.

**JAPAN**—**Byodo-in** (p. 176)—Ric Ergenbright/Corbis; (p. 177)—Getty Images; [p. 178 (upper: left & right), p. 179 (left)]—Michael S. Yamashita/Corbis; [p. 178 (lower), p. 179 (right)]—Archivo Iconografico, S.A./Corbis. **Kinkaku-ji** (p. 180)—Getty Images; [p. 181, p. 183 (upper far right & lower right)]—Photolibrary; (p. 182)—Ei Katsumata/World of Stock; [p. 183 (left)]—Archivo Iconografico, S.A./Corbis; [p. 183 (upper centre)]—iStockphoto.com/Ooyoo. **Saiho-ji** (p. 184)—Macduff Everton/Corbis; [p. 185, p. 186 (lower)]—Ric Ergenbright/Corbis; [p. 186 (upper left)]—B.S.P.I./Corbis; [p. 186 (upper right)]—Michael S. Yamashita/Corbis; [p. 187 (left)]—Gary Braasch/Corbis; [p. 187 (right)]—Photolibrary. **Kokyo Higashi Gyoen** [p. 1, p. 13 (lower right), p. 191 (centre right)]—Photolibrary; [pp. 134-135, p. 188, p. 189, p. 191 (upper, lower: left & right), p. 207]—Getty Images; (p. 190)—B.S.P.I./Corbis. **Kairaku-en** [p. 192, p. 193 (upper)]—Kylie Wilson/Positive Image Innovation; [p. 193 (lower: left & right)]—Photolibrary; [p. 194 (left), p. 195]—Getty Images; [p. 194 (right)]—Claire Takacs.

# BIBLIOGRAPHY

*Between Eden and Earth: Gardens of the Islamic World*, Islamic Arts Museum, Malaysia.

Asher, C. *"Gardens of the Nobility: Raja Man Singh and the Bagh-I-Wah"* In M. Hussain, A. Reman, J. Wescoat (eds.) *The Mughal Garden*, Lahore: Ferozsons 1996.

Brand, Michael. *"The Shahdara Gardens of Lahore"* In James L. Wescoat Jr. and Joachim Wolschke-Bulmahn (eds.) *Mughal Gardens: Sources, Representations, Places, and Prospects*, Washington, DC: Dumbarton Oaks, 1996.

Clarke, Emma *The Art of Islamic Gardens*, The Crowood Press Ltd., 2004.

Cole, H.H. *Tomb of Jahangir at Shahdara Near Lahore*, Calcutta, 1884.

Cox, Madison *Artists' Gardens*, Harry N. Abrams Inc., 1993.

Eraly, Abraham *The Mughal Throne: The Saga of India's Great Emperors*, Orionbooks, 2004.

Hattstein, Markus (ed.) & Delius, Peter (ed.) *Islam Art & Architecture*, Konemann, 2002.

Hobhouse, Penelope *The Story of Gardening*, DK Pub, 2002.

Itoh, Teiji *The Gardens of Japan*, Kudansha International Ltd., 1984.

Jinarajadasa, C, *Golden Book of the Theosophical Society*, Kessinger Publishing.

Keswick, Maggie *The Chinese Garden: History, Art and Architecture*, (ed.) A. Hardie, Harvard University Press, 2003.

Lala, Ramon Reyes *The Philippine Islands*, New York: Continental Publishing Company, 1899.

Lindquist, Carl, *Chandigarh and the Rock Garden*.

Maizels, John *Nek Chand's Wonder of the World*, Raw Creation, Phaidon Press.

Nitschke, Gunter *Japanese Gardens*, Taschen America Llc., 2007.

Quezon, Manuel L. III, Alcazaren, Paulo and Barns, Jeremy *Malacañan Palace: The Official Illustrated History*, Manila: Studio 5 Publishing, 2005.

Rehman, A. *Historic Towns of Punjab; Ancient and Medieval Period*, Lahore: Ferozsons, 1997.

Robinson, Francis *The Mughal Emperors and the Islamic Dynasties of India, Iran & Central Asia*, Thames & Hudson.

Seeling, C. Landau, C. Korda, C. *Happiness is a Garden*, Feierabend Verlag OHG, 2005.

Spencer-Jones, Rae *1001 Gardens You Must See Before You Die*, Cassell Illustrated, Octopus Publishing Group Limited.

Turner, Tom *Garden History Philosophy and Design, 2000 BC–2000 AD*, Taylor and Francis, 2005.

Valder, Peter *Gardens In China*, Timber Press Inc., 2002.

Vaughan, Philippa *The Mughal Garden at Hasan Abdal: A Unique Surviving Example of a 'Manzil' Bagh*.

Warren, William *The Tropical Garden*, Thames & Hudson, 2000.

Wescoat, James L., *"The Geographic Meaning of Shalamar Garden"* In *Shalamar Garden Lahore: Landscape, Form and Meaning*, Karachi: Pakistan Department of Archaeology, 1990.

Wescoat, James L. Jr., Michael Brand and M. Naeem Mir *The Shahdara Gardens of Lahore: Site Documentation and Spatial Analysis*, Pakistan Archaeology 25, 1990.

Wijaya, Made *Modern Tropical Garden Design*, Editions Didier Millet Pte. Ltd., 2007.

http://www.

agridept.gov.lk
archnet.org
bharatonline.com
bogor.indo.net.id
britannica.com
byodoin.or.jp
cdg.go.kr
chinaheritagenewsletter.org
chollipo.org
cwgc.org
gardenvisit.com
geocities.com
geographia.com
hoam.samsungfoundation.org
iaf.nl
imsc.res.in
indyahills.com
indiaprofile.com
infolanka.com
i-putra.com.my
japan-guide.com
javajones.worldpress.com
jktourism.org
jnto.go.jp
ksd.gov.hk
kunaicho.go.jp
laguna.net
lcsd.gov.hk
links.jstor.org
lipi.go.id
mughalgardens.org
nekchand.com
nekchand.info
nongnoochtropicalgarden.com
nparks.gov.sg
op.gov.ph
orientalarchitecture.com
pakistan.gov.pk
pref.ibaraki.lg.jp
ptwijaya.com
qsbg.org
rajasthantourism.gov.in
rawvision.com
sabah.net.my

sbg.org.sg
skill.hrd.korea.or.kr
soswaewon.org
thebeijingguide.com
tirtagangga.nl
tour2korea.com
tourism.gov.pk
travelchinaguide.com
ts-adyar.org
udaipurtourism.com
uplb.edu.ph
web-japan.org
webindia123.com
whc.unesco.org
wikipedia.org
yamasa.org
zoo.com.sg

# INDEX